Managing
the
Corporate Image

Managing the Corporate Image

THE KEY TO PUBLIC TRUST

JAMES G. GRAY, JR.

Quorum Books
Westport, Connecticut · London, England

Library of Congress Cataloging-in-Publication Data

Gray, James G.
    Managing the corporate image.

    Bibliography: p.
    Includes index.
    1. Corporate image.   2. Industry—
Social aspects.   I. Title.
HD59.2.G7   1986   658.4   85-9598
ISBN 0-89930-140-1 (lib. bdg. : alk. paper)

Library of Congress Catalog Card Number: 85-9598
ISBN: 0-89930-140-1

First published in 1986 by Quorum Books

Greenwood Press
A division of Congressional Information Service, Inc.
88 Post Road West, Westport, Connecticut 06881

Printed in the United States of America

∞

The paper used in this book complies with the
Permanent Paper Standard issued by the National
Information Standards Organization (Z39.48-1984).

10 9 8 7 6 5 4 3 2 1

Copyright Acknowledgments

The publisher and author are grateful to the following for granting the use of their material:

Lippincott & Margulies, Inc., New York, N.Y. "Reality and Perception," *Sense 82,* May 1981. Reprinted with special permission.

Material reprinted from the January 22, 1979 issue of Business Week by special permission, © 1979 by McGraw-Hill, Inc., New York, N.Y. 10020. All rights reserved.

Interview with Lawrence G. Foster printed with permission of Lawrence G. Foster, Corporate Vice President, Public Relations, Johnson & Johnson.

Interview with Raymond L. Hoewing printed with permission of Raymond L. Hoewing, Vice President, Public Affairs Council, Washington, D.C.

Written interview and materials supplied by Henry Spier reprinted with permission of Atlantic Richfield Company.

Written interview materials supplied by Mary D. Sellars reprinted with permission of Mary D. Sellars, PR Officer, Sovran Bank, NA.

Interview materials supplied by Odonna Mathews reprinted with permission of Odonna Mathews, Vice President of Consumer Affairs, Giant Food, Inc.

Interview with Irene M. Brandt printed with permission of Irene M. Brandt.

Excerpts from the Cox Report reprinted with permission from *Advertising Age,* October 25, 1982, copyright CRAIN Communications, Inc., 1982.

Excerpts from Craig E. Aranoff and Otis W. Baskin, *Public Relations: The Profession and the Practice* (St. Paul, Minn.: West Publishing Co., 1983) reprinted with permission of West Publishing Company.

Contents

Part III. Measuring Impact

Preface

Why does the reputation of one company remain sound while the reputation of another falters? Long-standing, successful companies know that their image for producing quality goods and services, and for hiring managers who respond to employee and community needs and work closely with the government and media, enables them to succeed.

A corporate image consists of the essential qualities attributed to the corporation. It is formed in the minds of employees, customers, investors, the media, government, and citizens. A corporate image is a composite of people's attitudes and beliefs about that corporation. All actions, all products, all pronouncements of the corporation convey signals and generate messages that contribute to public perception.

Corporate reality and public perception are often miles apart. Indeed, the corporate-publics relationship presents a paradox. On one side of the coin, the public expects business to provide society with sound economic underpinnings while leading institutions toward an improved social order. On the other side, these same publics express distrust of big business and its leaders. Expanding profits, nonconcerned managers and lack of social responsibility are the reasons most often cited.

Corporate image is one link between corporate reality and public perception. A corporate image program that responds openly and consistently builds public trust. A primary concern of all business is to strengthen public trust. And that's a major reason why I have written *Managing the Corporate Image:* to provide business leaders with guidelines for defining, setting up, administering and evaluating a corporate image program.

Managing the Corporate Image combines my expertise as a communication and image consultant with experience drawn from other experts in the business arena, reinforced with case studies, research and surveys. For those who question the number of sources cited, keep in mind that image is still viewed askance in some circles. Substantiation from expert sources is one indication of the growth of corporate image as a tool to establish trust and credibility.

Managing the Corporate Image is the sequel to my first book, *The Winning Image*. The two provide a compendium of the internal/external corporate image function.

To get the most out of the book, begin at the beginning. Chapter 1 defines corporate image and explains why it is a vital concern for business leaders. Chapter 2 briefly recaps events from the past few decades that have led to diminished public confidence and the resulting deflated corporate image. Chapters 3 and 4 offer examples of corporations' working image programs. Chapters 5 through 11 are devoted to advice for establishing your own corporate image program, and contain additional real-life examples reinforced with how-to information. Chapter 12 helps you form your own corporate image profile.

Acknowledgments

A special word of gratitude to Judy Baird and Henry Spier, Atlantic Richfield Company; Lawrence G. Foster, Johnson & Johnson; Odonna Mathews, Giant Food; Mary D. Sellars, Sovran Bank, N. A.; Irene Brandt, Eli Lilly and Co.; and Raymond Hoewing, the Public Affairs Council; for the interviews and materials they so graciously shared to make this work possible.

PART I

The Corporate Image Concept

1

What Is Corporate Image and Why Is It an Important Concern for Business Leaders?

IBM . . . Xerox . . . Johnson & Johnson . . . GE . . . ARCO . . . NBC . . . PanAm . . . Like a word-association game, we form mental images of these corporations as though they possess lifelike attributes. Whether the image provoked in our minds represents company products, its logo, its chief executive officer, or a news event associated with the company, we all have some notion of a corporation's "being." The personification of corporations is most evident in the positive or negative image corporations portray. But like all living creatures, corporate reputations soar, falter, plunge, and soar again.

Corporate managers are beginning to realize the importance of corporate image. A strong, positive image can see a corporation through a crisis as in the case of the Tylenol crisis at Johnson & Johnson, or through a period of red ink as in the case of Chrysler. Sovran Bank recognized the importance of image early in the merger of two banks to form a new bank. Bank executives understood that an appropriate, well-planned image attracts top-notch personnel, it attracts customers, and it attracts investors—three key ingredients in creating a successful business. Atlantic Richfield management likewise realized its image might have become linked to a negative "big oil" public perception and so corrected this problem, largely through an aggressive communications effort to directly address public concerns. These image-building programs, detailed in the pages of this book, cite just a few major corporations whose images play a vital role in their corporate lives. Just as a corporation appears to be a living, breathing being, just as it develops a "personality," it must guard against allowing that personality to become misinterpreted or misunderstood. It must gain and hold public goodwill in order to succeed economically and even physically. Corporate leaders have begun to realize that they cannot allow public goodwill to evaporate and then become replaced by hostility. They must preserve and nurture positive public opinion as if it were the company's most valued asset.

On the surface, the image of corporate giants stands for success, quality, and credibility. In fact, the outward symbol may be so firmly emblazoned in our minds, we forget the name hidden underneath. We simply associate IBM with computers, Xerox with office copy machines, and Johnson & Johnson with baby oil.

When we dig deeper, we turn up a reputation for substantive business goals—to compete and survive in a capitalistic society, to provide jobs, to manufacture and sell a product or service, to represent the best of the profit motive, to support the national and world economies, and to contribute to the well-being of human kind.

Why does the image of one company remain steady while the image of another appears shaky? Successful companies know that public perception is part myth and part reality. To separate myth from reality, a company manages its image projected to the many publics with which it is in contact. Managing the corporate image is the key to securing and maintaining public trust. The consumer relies on the company for quality goods and services. Employees feel that their jobs are not in jeopardy. Media rely on company leaders for open communication. Government/business relations are well planned and consistent. The general public perceives the corporate reputation as solid and secured in reality. Business leaders who guide and shape the corporate reality safeguard the image by openly and honestly communicating with these publics.

THE DEVELOPMENT OF THE CORPORATE IMAGE

Yet corporate image is more than the product of the phenomenon of mob psychology. Corporate image results not so much from a single attitude held by the public at large, but from a mosaic of attitudes formed in the minds of those in close contact with the corporation. Corporate image formation begins with those inside the organization. Those on the inside include, foremost, employees. The image employees form spills into the community and spreads beyond with a rippling effect. The community, consumers, suppliers, investors, and finally the media and the government cause the organization's image to permeate throughout society, which subliminally absorbs it. Those inside and outside the corporation constitute small publics whose interactions with the corporation contribute to the total image picture. At the most basic level of doing business, these publics decide if a corporation is credible and economically stable and if it produces quality products and reliable services.

On the surface, employees view the corporation merely as a provider of jobs. They depend on the corporation for economic stability, self-pride,

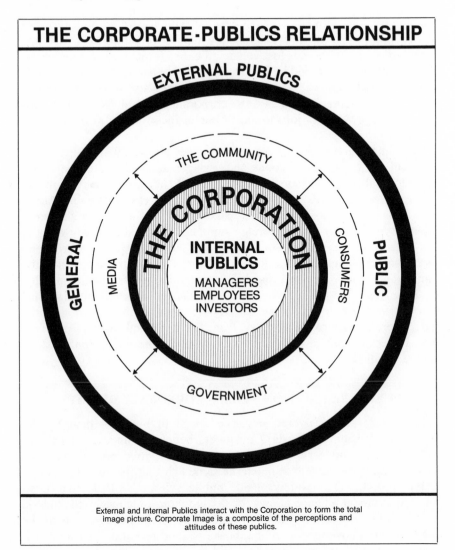

THE CORPORATE-PUBLICS RELATIONSHIP

EXTERNAL PUBLICS

THE COMMUNITY

THE CORPORATION

INTERNAL PUBLICS

MANAGERS
EMPLOYEES
INVESTORS

GENERAL

MEDIA

CONSUMERS

PUBLIC

GOVERNMENT

External and Internal Publics interact with the Corporation to form the total image picture. Corporate Image is a composite of the perceptions and attitudes of these publics.

and the ability to plan for the future. Should the corporation falter, their lives are directly affected. Recent steel plant closings in which employees in Pittsburgh, Pennsylvania, and Weirton, West Virginia, suddenly found themselves without jobs, provide an example. Former plant employees, upon learning about the closings, felt abandoned by employers. They expressed their resentment with hostility toward management and "The Corporation."

Employee feelings filtered into the community creating widespread hostility. Because high unemployment meant loss of revenues for the community, the community itself reacted with frustrated anger toward the corporation. Hostility magnified while the community's lifeblood withered. Citizens' homes lost value and banks foreclosed on mortgages. Community leaders stood by helplessly as entire towns were abandoned, schools and churches closed, and local govenments were left without decision makers. Needless to say, the corporate image shifted from a positive one as provider of jobs to one of big business out for profit and self-interest.

Consumer perceptions of corporate image, on the other hand, take a different slant. Buyers of goods and services demand that corporations provide quality at a reasonable cost and that they back quality with reliable service. Failures by corporations in these areas often cause American consumers to lose faith. In retaliation, buyers appeal to consumer advocacy groups or turn to foreign suppliers. For instance, the woes of the Detroit automakers are blamed on the industry's failure to respond to consumer demands for reliable, economic transportation. Once the American public perceived that the automobile industry had responded to these needs by shifting to smaller cars backed with extended service warranties, the favorable image of Detroit automakers revived. In large part, a profit turnaround resulted from the improved image. American auto buyers perceived that the Detroit manufacturers had their best interests in mind.

PUBLIC PERCEPTION VERSUS CORPORATE REALITY

Nevertheless, the overall negative image of business held by the American consumer persists. Consumers believe businesses emphasize quality goods and services too little. In fact, public perception casts business and government in much the same light, pitting both against the public good. The widely held public view is that the business/government alliance allows for tax loopholes, high-salaried leaders, influence buyers, and expanding profits. The public believes it is at the mercy of both government and big business. And recent occurrences such as the war in Vietnam, Watergate, and the Arab oil embargo crystallize public opinion firmly against trusting government and business.

In many cases, the media feed this negative public view. Television newscasts seize upon a misdeed, painting a negative image to reinforce already existing negative perceptions. The net result is a mosaic of public attitudes that demonstrate an unfavorable image for corporate America. Indeed, the corporation appears to be a bull's-eye target surrounded by publics which remain ready to shoot at the slightest misbehavior.

To turn this perception around, corporations need a continuous public image campaign that openly and honestly communicates with each of these publics, including employees, consumers, and investors, and which responds readily to their concerns. Stop-gap measures providing temporary remedies are not enough. Responding only after a rude awakening, such as a media exposé or an employee or consumer lawsuit, is a poor substitute for sound image-building policies. The successful corporation relies on long-term efforts to secure and hold favorable public perception. Constant reevaluation of the image provides the corporation a mechanism to communicate with the public and to safeguard the corporate image.

The Perception Gap

A *New York Times* article recently noted

a widespread perception that it is not just shareholders who are being let down by a deterioration in ethical behavior in business and on Wall Street, but corporations themselves, the economy, and even the public at large—in the sense that a society needs to feel there is some fairness in the business system and some sense of stewardship in its leaders.[1]

Public misperception of business is discussed in *Sense 82*, a publication distributed to 15,000 business leaders by Lippincott & Margulies, Inc., a New York communications, marketing and design firm: "If your company is misperceived, you are not alone. Corporations everywhere have been having an increasingly vexsome time getting their important publics to see them as they really are."

Sense 82 cites these reasons, among others, for the widening gap between corporate reality and public misperception:

- Disappearance of the one-product company and rise of the diversified corporation;
- Waves of mergers, acquisitions, and takeovers; corporate identity crises; and communication problems;
- Bewildering array of media options—and their rising costs;
- Shifting demographics; new and rapidly evolving lifestyles; and the new and different ways of perceiving companies, products, and services;
- Inability of managements to perceive the reality of their own corporation and its relationship to the changing marketplace.

Corporate image is the key to understanding and reacting to the public demand for corporate social responsibility and to providing the link between public perception and corporate reality. The goal of a corporate image program is to bring perception into line with reality. As *Sense 82* correctly observes, "Not even the most costly advertising or public relations efforts will bring into sharp focus the identities of corporations" without first responding to the challenge of creating "a clear and positive identity, based on corporate reality—on what the corporation is, where it wants to go, and how it plans to get there."

Sense 82 concludes:

Management can, as farsighted leaders among them have demonstrated, bring perception more closely into line with reality. They can work to assure that the images formed by all their publics are accurately relfected in benefits and positive contributions to the business community and to the consumer.[2]

PUBLIC IMAGE: A GROWING CORPORATE CONCERN

How people view a company is vital to that company's success. Corporations have long realized the marketplace value of polishing the image of their products. Now they have to package and sell themselves as well. How a company is perceived affects the bottom line, directly influencing the morale and attitudes of investors, lenders of capital, and even the finance ministries of foreign countries where the company wants to do business. However, a favorable public image is central to the achievement of other corporate goals.

Building and communicating the corporate image has become a major concern for businesses and business leaders. Accountability to the media's watchful eye causes business to pay close attention to public perception.

To illustrate the growing concern for corporate image, *Fortune* surveyed nearly 6,000 executives, outside directors, and financial analysts, asking them to rate the reputations of the ten largest companies in the twenty largest industries in the United States.

The *Fortune* survey drew responses from 51 percent of those polled— an unusually enthusiastic response, according to polling professionals. The industries represented in the survey are the largest in *Fortune*'s directories of U.S. industrial and nonindustrial corporations. The companies in each industry category were rated on eight main attributes:

1. Quality of management
2. Quality of products or services
3. Innovativeness
4. Value as a long-term investment
5. Financial soundness
6. Ability to attract and keep talented people
7. Community and environmental responsibility
8. Use of corporate assets

The significance of the survey is that, first, corporations were rated on reputation—that is, the perception of important publics including executives, outside directors, and financial analysts. Second, virtually every attribute is associated with how the company looks to outsiders.

Most significantly, these attributes contribute directly to the perceived corporate image. Quality of management; quality of products or services; ability to attract, develop, and keep talented people (internal corporate image); and community and environmental responsibility serve as major themes throughout the following chapters.

The image or reputation of the well-thought-of companies appears tied to their financial standing. According to the *Fortune* survey results:

Well-thought-of companies generally do well in financial terms too, and those with poor reputations do poorly. Four companies on the honor roll—IBM, GE, Merck, and AT&T—have triple-A bond ratings. Three others—SmithKline Beckman, General Mills, and Digital Equipment—are rated double-A.[3]

Interestingly enough, the *Fortune* survey was conducted before someone packed cyanide into Tylenol capsules in Chicago, killing seven people. Yet the incident seems to have had little lasting effect on the reputation of Johnson & Johnson, Tylenol's maker and the case study for Chapter 3. One indicator (and others are pointed out in Chapter 3) which demonstrates this point is that Johnson & Johnson stock returned to pre-crisis levels within months after the incident and in early December 1982 reached $49 a share, a record high.

All the companies on the *Fortune* honor roll have chief executives who have been with their companies at least twenty years. In sharp contrast, eight of the ten companies rated lowest have hired, fired, or otherwise rearranged top management in the recent past. Respondents seemed to equate poor corporate performance with poor management.

Almost all the highly rated companies stress motivating—and retaining—their most promising managers by allowing them freedom to make decisions within a few broad policy guidelines.

As the *Fortune* article author, Claire Makin, points out:

Reputation can assume as many shapes as Proteus, the Greek sea god, and be as difficult to pin down. But when Michael Geran of E. F. Hutton was asked why IBM is so well thought of, he replied that the company's reputation rests on accomplishment. "Perception is reality," he says. *Fortune's* survey suggests that this claim, argued by philosophers through the ages, isn't far off the mark.

The top corporations listed in the *Fortune* survey, rated on eight key attributes of reputation, follow:

- Quality of management
  1. IBM
  2. Hewlett-Packard
  3. Johnson & Johnson

- Quality of products and services
  1. Boeing
  2. Caterpillar Tractor
  3. Hewlett-Packard

- Innovativeness
  1. Citicorp
  2. Merrill Lynch
  3. Hewlett-Packard

- Long-term investment value
  1. IBM
  2. Hewlett-Packard
  3. Johnson & Johnson

- Financial soundness
  1. IBM
  2. American Home Products
  3. Johnson & Johnson

- Ability to attract, develop, and keep talented people
  1. Hewlett-Packard
  2. IBM
  3. Merck

- Community and environmental responsibility
  1. Eastman Kodak
  2. IBM
  3. Johnson & Johnson

- Use of corporate assets
  1. Johnson & Johnson
  2. IBM
  3. Abbott Laboratories

Examples of the concern for corporate image abound. One recent example is the breakup of American Telephone & Telegraph (AT&T). A business giant, AT&T broke into twenty-two wholly owned telephone companies with seven regional holding companies. Corporate image received high priority in the divestiture process. Brian O'Reilly, business observer and author, points out that the reorganization caused the smaller companies to develop unique and contrasting personalities. The western region was the first to create a new name, US West, now striving for an exciting new image to attract new investors. NYNEX, the northeast regional company, will depend on its image of steady performance.[4]

Finance and banking concerns are experiencing similar efforts to change images. Financial observer and author Russell Anspach cites increasing consumer sophistication as a major impetus for banks to change their images. "The emerging awareness of the importance of identity," says Anspach, "can be gauged by the growing number of name changes in the banking industry. Since 1980, some 895 banks and financial institutions have changed their names."[5]

Concern for public image has reached the developing high technology arena. Since 1973, TRW Corporation, a major producer of automotive parts, electronic components, oilfield equipment, and spacecraft, has spent over $35 million on corporate advertising and has vastly improved its public recognition. A benchmark study conducted in 1973 showed little public recognition of the company. In a subsequent campaign to improve the TRW image, two audiences were targeted in the image-enhancement program—those who affect decisions for buying stocks by institutions and individual investors, and those who affect buying decisions of TRW products. The campaign focused on the company's philosophy about managing information and technology. Familiarity with TRW increased 40 percent from the base after the first eighteen months.[6]

Besides consumers, however, corporations rely on favorable images to attract investors. The weight carried by corporate image into the financial community was revealed in a study of Wall Street investment decisions. The report disclosed that corporate image is far from intangible—it is a big factor in investment selection. General Electric's image as "aggressive in product research" and IBM's image of "product and marketing excellence" were cited by analysts as examples of images that win investors' consideration. Because people are clearly influenced by corporate image, the financial analyst must reckon with it, too.

Creating and maintaining favorable public visibility is a main concern of big business. What the public believes about a corporation determines, in many cases, whether or not the business succeeds. Large oil companies, the insurance industry, airlines, public service and sales organizations, even the federal government, spend millions of dollars each year to safeguard their public images.

Knowing how to influence public opinion builds a favorable business environment and is required of businesses if they are to continue. In a special report to *Business Week* Loet A. Velmans, president of Hill and Knowlton, the nation's largest public relations firm, warns that corporate survival is increasingly difficult: "The corporation faces intensified competition in the marketplace, the growing threat of takeover by outsiders, and new challenges in employee relations. And all the while, the corporate community continues to be plagued by a negative public image."

Velmans goes on to say that, in order to survive, corporations are working harder to project a better public image:

The corporation is being politicized and has assumed another dimension in our society that it did not have as recently as 10 years ago. As a result, the corporation has become more conscious of using communications to reach its objectives, and it is articulating its position more clearly to government agencies, legislators, shareholders, employees, customers, financial institutions, and other critical audiences.[7]

WHY IS CORPORATE IMAGE A VITAL CONCERN FOR BUSINESS LEADERS?

Chicago management consultant Allan Cox, in his study called *The Cox Report on the American Corporation*, concludes that business leaders appear isolated from society. Cox writes:

Despite business executives having developed reputations as men of action, they are embarrassingly uninformed about the social environment in which they live and move. . . . Social environment here refers not only to the publics (both domestic and foreign) that corporations serve, but to the whole human, interpersonal webwork that forms our corporations themselves, as well as our society at large, which has a future to be shaped.

In the three-year study, Cox conducted a nationwide survey of 115 operating units in thirteen leading American corporations. Survey results were tallied from an over 400-item questionnaire distributed to 1,086 top- and middle-management executives. An undeniable and disturbing theme emerged from the significant 93 percent return of the questionnaires. According to the study, "Corporations, and their executives, tend not to know what kind of engagement with society is required of them to meet their own goals, and they seem not to want to know."

The study reveals additional significant observations:

- Only one-fifth of the respondents believe it is important to articulate their corporations' needs to the public.
- Although they seek positive community images, only 21 percent of top executives and 18 percent of the middle group say their companies place much importance on making known their interests to community publics.
- Only half the responding executives believe providing goods and services is important.

Cox concludes:

Many corporations maintain perspectives that render them unrelated to their communities. For them, it's as if the world were a jigsaw puzzle and their existence confined to one piece of the puzzle, having no dependence on any other pieces; their executives suffer from tunnel vision. Achievements and objectives concerning affairs of business alone are all they can see. . . .

The mindset of corporations also is displayed in educating the public. Though companies seek positive images in their communities, they are reticent about making known their requirements to them. Only 21 percent of top executives and 18 percent of middle ones say their companies put very much or most importance on doing so. Few companies perform well at this.[8]

Corporate image should remain a concern to managers for several diverse reasons. First, failure to respond to public pressures can mean the downfall of the entire corporation. Employees blame management for what goes wrong. Dissatisfaction among employees translates to low morale, low productivity, high absenteeism, and other losses. Dissatisfaction among consumers translates to unsold products, directly reducing profits. And a tarnished image viewed by investors results in loss of revenues for capital outlay.

A second reason revolves around management's short-term orientation toward profit. Management's view must shift toward long-term concerns including producing quality products, aiding employees in career development, integrating the corporate culture with that of the community in which it conducts business, and working with the local media and governments. Repeated criticism of business leaders reflects the attitude that business leaders' only concerns center on next quarter's profits. Along with profit motives, business leaders must give equal consideration to the emerging corporate culture and social concerns. Business now operates in an environment that demands accountability beyond the annual report. Employees are no longer happy with a paycheck and an occasional pat on the back. They want an active role in shaping corporate policy. They want profit sharing, stock options, staggered hours, and other benefits.

Likewise, customers want quality products and they place renewed demands on management to produce quality or be aware that the consumer is prepared to seek support from groups who will ensure that demands are met. Should the dissatisfied consumer seek redress, business leaders may find themselves face-to-face with consumer advocates, television cameras, or government regulatory agencies.

In defining the role of the manager in future years, managers must understand the existing paradox. The trends shaping the future corporate culture, and the forces that have shaped the corporate culture for the past quarter century or more, require managers to reduce the gulf between the corporation and the publics on which they depend for economic survival.

The responsibility for defining and building the corporate image must become a major management concern. A priority item on the agenda of managers of the next decade must be to shorten the gap between corporate reality and public perception. Business leaders must be able to perceive the reality of their own corporation and its relationship to the changing marketplace.

The standard management attitude is naturally geared toward the profit figure. The manager is the guardian of profit, performance, personnel, and potential. If all goes well, credibility is assumed safe. This traditional philosophy works for day-to-day operation. But for maintaining overall corporate health, something is missing. The missing element is public perception, how the public views the corporation. To begin an image-building program, managers must be willing to step back and objectively put themselves in the shoes of the public. Doing so requires defining public concerns and responding with a corporate image program to communicate openly and honestly with the public. A second step is to be willing to bring public perception into line with corporate reality. What the manager sees as reality can and must mesh with what the public perceives.

As the Cox study points out, "It is a corporation's responsibility that citizens be educated about its business problems and conditions. As the public and corporations share in the same problems and if these two become aware of their interdependence, they will add to each other's understanding."[9]

NOTES

1. Ann Crittenden, "The Age of 'Me-First' Management," *New York Times*, August 19, 1984, p. 1.

2. Lippincott & Margulies, Inc., "Reality and Perception," *Sense 82*, May 1981.

3. Claire Makin, "Ranking Corporate Reputations," *Fortune* 107 (January 10, 1983): 34–44.

4. Brian O'Reilly, "Ma Bell's Kids Fight for Position," *Fortune* 107 (June 27, 1983): 62–68.

5. Russell Anspach, "Corporate Identity: Bank Marketing Power for the 80s," *National Association of Bank Women's Journal* 59 (July/August 1983): 13–18.

6. George Bonner, Jr., "Building Image for a Company Called TRW," *Madison Avenue Magazine* 25 (Feburary 1983): 60–63.

7. Reprinted from *Business Week* (January 22, 1979): by special permission. All rights reserved.

8. Allan Cox, "Where executives fall short," *Advertising Age* (Oct. 25, 1982): 00–62.

9. Ibid., p. 62.

2

The Emerging Corporation: Public Outcry for Social Responsibility

Business is being criticized and called a bum today for doing the same things that made it a hero just a few years ago. Business hasn't changed; society has changed. The period from the end of World War II to the late nineteen-sixties was a time when what people wanted and what business provided were perfectly synchronized. What has happened since is that the values of the country have shifted.

Leonard Silk and David Vogel
*Ethics and Profits: The Crisis of Confidence
in American Business*[1]

The public has become the corporate mirror. The corporate reflection may be unflattering, even ugly, due to public loss of confidence. Just how distorted the picture has become is demonstrated in a public opinion poll conducted by Yankelovich, Skelly and White. They asked people just how well business strikes a balance between profit and the public interest. In 1967, the results placed the public confidence level at about 70 percent. In 1981, the level had dropped to 19 percent.

The dramatically lowered esteem of business must be viewed in light of the public's loss of confidence in all institutions, not just business alone. Traditionally, society has relied on established institutions to pave the way for change and to bring that change about. Schools and colleges provided education leading to better jobs and an improved lifestyle. Government and its leaders represented the people and protected their best interests. The church was the bastion of faith and love. The family could be depended on in a time of need.

The last 100 years have seen American society pass through at least three revolutions, from an agrarian to an industrial to a technological society. World wars and the availability of nuclear weapons make us conscious, for the first time, that the human race can become extinct. The potential end of civilization permeates the world mind.

The invention and pervasiveness of television and computers have changed the way we communicate, allowing instant global communication. Computers are deemed a breakthrough as important as learning to write. Supersonic jets make it possible to cross continents and oceans within hours.

The net result of these complex forces is the creation of a fluid, mobile society of overpowering size, impersonality, and interdependence.

FROM A SOCIETY OF INSTITUTIONS TO A SOCIETY OF PUBLICS

These forces are producing a change in the values society places in institutions. The change can be observed in the family, the church, the education system, the government, and in business.

For example, the values placed in the family reflect the change. In the past, the agrarian family tended to be large and close-knit and existed as a self-sufficient economic unit. Each family member was expected to contribute to the unit to reap rewards. When the family changed from an agrarian, economic unit to a smaller, less dependent, industrial unit, a parallel change in values took place. The shift to an industrial base saw the family institution give way to dependency upon the corporation for economic survival and security. The corporation provided economic rewards and allowed for upward mobility defined as success.

Faith in education provides another example. The agrarian child largely ignored higher education, depending on the land for self-support. With the move to town and the factory job, the industrial child entered schools and colleges as a means to climb the social and success ladder. Discovering that a college degree does not guarantee job success and upward mobility, today's youths view technological training as the key to education. Because technical preparedness is the current springboard to personal and business success, computer and electronics schools are overrun with students.

The shift in values placed in institutions has led to their restructure. In the extreme, some argue, we are experiencing the complete breakdown of institutions. Families are no longer neat packages of working father, homemaker mother, and loving children. Single parents and unmarried couples rear children, and some parents put career success as a first priority. Moreover, the education system is perceived as faltering as society discovers its high school graduates cannot read and write. And teachers who traditionally provided the moral underpinnings of society now strike for higher salaries or leave teaching altogether. In political circles, voter apathy reflects the loss of faith in government and its leaders. Church and synagogue attendance ebbs or soars, reacting to public moods.

Likewise, as an institution, the American corporation has undergone a shift in the values placed in it. The dramatic loss of public confidence has already been discussed. Additionally, corporations seek alternative structures giving high priority to employee ownership and input, decreasing the managerial role. Employees who want personal rewards beyond a paycheck now join corporations as a stepping-stone to the next rung of success.

As an American institution, the emerging corporation must take its cultural environment into consideration. The corporation of the 1980s and beyond will operate in a social/cultural environment, not just in an economic environment, a fact largely ignored until recent years.

The lesson to be learned is that institutions and the society they serve have undergone dramatic change. In past years, the link between institutions and society was direct and dependent. To accomplish a goal, people worked within established institutions. Now people work outside established institutions, tending to ally with population segments to accomplish goals and to pressure institutions to change or become aware of their concerns.

Against this backdrop, efforts to improve public attitudes must address the credibility of corporations, showing concern for individuals on a human scale, helping the public to understand economic realities, and leading society toward change. The point is underscored by business author Edward Newfeld who explains:

The current relationship between enterprise and society is still undergoing change. Neither the character of the enterprise nor that of society is static, and each corporation interfaces with society in different ways. Over time, society has reacted to the enterprise. The enterprise is a unique entity with distinct social responsibilities and a collective conscience, and its social legitimacy depends on its ability to provide society with its material needs. In relation to social matters, when the enterprise acts with a view to maintaining its long-term validity, its actions tend to reflect the social outlook of the nation in general, thus providing testimony to an interdependent relationship between corporate behavior and social values.[2]

The business community's concern with the public's faith contains an important insight—that a society cannot function well without public confidence in its institutions and its leaders. In the United States, large corporations and their executives become critical elements in a healthy and stable social order. It makes a big difference whether the institutions that dominate a society exercise authority according to legitimate claims or whether the public regards corporate roles as improper or illegitimate.

The business community has every reason to be concerned about the American public's lack of confidence in it. And the challenge now facing America's executives is not to explain themselves better, but to demonstrate that they take the public's concerns and criticisms seriously.

Historical Framework Since 1950

Discovery of the growing chasm between business and the public is fairly recent, falling roughly within the past thirty-five years. A National Industrial Conference Board report concludes that the 1950s were a period when most Americans viewed the business community with relative trust and respect. America seemed quite content with business as a major employer and provider of goods and services. There was little need for a corporation to explain itself, let alone justify itself to its stakeholders.[3]

Those returning from World War II to enter the work force enjoyed the opportunities a stable and growing economy presented. The economy of the early 1950s turned from a war base to one of early developing technology. The auto industry took off as war men married, started families, and became mobile America. Housing boomed as families settled. Families increased the need for services, education, and health care alongside the demand for products. The seemingly idyllic Eisenhower days launched the nation on nearly a decade of respite from war and set in motion the end of the Industrial Revolution and the beginning of the technological era.

The Kennedy occupation of the White House signalled the end of the idyllic. The media became a major factor in shifting the focus of the American mind from an idyllic Camelot America to one of realities. Kennedy's assassination, the civil rights movement, the escalation of the war in Vietnam, and later the Watergate scandal coincided with the time when the media—television, in particular—began to exert its muscle. The shock of Kennedy's assassination, viewed publicly by millions, closely followed by the deportation of thousands to a far-off Vietnamese jungle, jolted the American public into a new reality. As baby boomers graduated from high school in the mid-1960s, the idea of another war was abhorrent, especially an unexplained war.

The American public turned to previously trusted institutions such as the federal government for answers. But the government was caught in its own credibility crisis. It was attempting to fight an unpopular war in Vietnam—a struggle the government repeatedly denied by not declaring war. And with Watergate soon after, it became increasingly clear that elected government officials were lawbreakers. The natural reaction was distrust, often to the point of open hostility in the form of mass protests.

A generation reared under the soft guise of economic prosperity rejected the very institutions that provided the good times in the first place. Sons and daughters rebelled, adopting lifestyles and dress in open revolt against the establishment. Long hair became the symbol of a generation devoted to retaliation. San Francisco, New York, London, and Amsterdam became centers of counter culture as the American mood moved away from the cushiony crew-cut to embrace the counterrevolution immortalized in the music of the Beatles and the shock-producing rock opera *Hair*.

Yet social and cultural changes, the rise of civil rights, and rejection of an unjustifiable war went largely unnoticed by corporate America. Spurred by military spending and continuing advances in technology, big business remained detached. Reaction was minimal. Corporations felt the pressure from a national mood of rising expectations and responded simply by projecting a "good citizen" role.[4]

Throughout the 1960s, business leaders became involved in social and cultural issues to protect the corporate "good citizen" image. Businesses encouraged employees to become involved in community relations and to assume leadership positions. Corporations adopted an "enlightened self-interest in community affairs."[5]

As Vietnam took its toll, as college classrooms spilled over, as the resulting war wealth became flagrant, the national public splintered into subgroups. Some pursued anew the pleasure of wealth, others rejected profit for the commune.

The 1970s brought Watergate and President Nixon's ultimate resignation. Watergate signalled the final burst of the innocent bubble of trust the public had placed in its leaders. This one event, perhaps more than any before or since, affected the perception of and trust placed in previously unquestioned American institutions. Business felt the brunt. Arthur White and Madelyn Hochstein wrote, "The country experienced a widespread shift away from the ethic of self-sacrifice and hard work for future reward to the pursuit of self-fulfillment, immediate gratification, and personal involvement."[6]

The 1970s oil embargoes further damaged the business image, fueling public mistrust of big oil companies. The public felt betrayed as gasoline prices quadrupled while oil company profits doubled and tripled. Public concern continues as Middle East oil countries battle, leaving imported oil supplies uncertain. As a stop-gap measure, U.S. oil storage can sustain the nation for only a few months at best should a crisis arise. Meanwhile, government and business have seemingly abandoned a policy to guarantee long-term solutions.

Yet, while the nation finds itself faced with an energy crisis, business and government, in the public's view, waver between helplessness and unconcern. Government and business leaders apparently view nuclear energy sources as an alternative to reduce dependency on foreign oil, but Three Mile Island shocked the public mind out of its complacency about the safety and cost-effectiveness of nuclear energy.

Environmental concerns further damage corporate reputations. Toxic chemicals and hazardous wastes became a major issue when the Love Canal story broke. Although air and water pollution is a primary concern to virtually every American household in the 1980s, the government has responded with a weakened Environmental Protection Agency riddled with scandal which resulted in the toppling of its top administrators. Likewise, the controversial Department of Interior secretary, whose environmental policies were themselves questionable, eventually was forced to resign.

While the late 1970s brought double-digit inflation and interest rates as well as high unemployment figures, the mid-1980s find a faltering stock market caused by public concerns that the economic recovery is only temporary. The culprit for public nervousness is the huge government deficit. And one cause of the deficit is, in the public's view, defense spending in which many corporations are directly involved. Fat government contracts allow manufacturers of defense-related products to charge exorbitant prices for nuts and bolts found in local hardware stores for fractions of the price the military pays.

And as the economy struggles back to recovery, labor is asked to suffer cuts in pay and benefits only to find months later that as corporate finances improve, executives are given large bonuses running into seven-digit figures or more.

What emerges is a cynical public. The American public, once inclined to believe what it was told by business and government leaders, has grown skeptical, distrustful, and frustrated. Both business and government are now attempting to regain public trust, but the chasm is wide.

The image of alienation and mistrust bears grave significance for the American corporation and its leaders. Corporations do not exist in a vacuum; they are dynamic forces interacting with and shaping culture. To regain public trust, the corporation must view itself from the perspective of the cultural and social environment in which it exists.

A main goal of American business must be restoration of public trust. One link between the corporation and the public is the corporate image. But a sharp logo, expensive offices, and high-paid executives are not enough. A credible, sound, clear, continuing dialogue between public concerns and corporate claim must be apparent to today's sophisticated public. Corporate image is the key to restoring public trust and to guiding society toward an improved human condition.

NOTES

1. Leonard Silk and David Vogel, *Ethics and Profits: The Crisis of Confidence in American Business* (New York: Simon & Schuster, 1976).

2. *Public Relations Journal*, August 1982.

3. The National Industrial Conference Board, "The Role of Business in Public Affairs" (New York, 1968).

4. Ibid.

5. Charles M. Darling, III, and Thomas J. Diviney, "Business in Public Affairs Today," *Public Affairs in National Focus* (New York: Knopf, 1980), p. 141.

6. Arthur H. White and Madelyn Hochstein, "The Climate for Business in the 1980s: New Challenges, New Opportunities," in *Business and Society: Strategies for the 1980s* (Washington D.C.: U.S. Dept. of Commerce, 1980), p. 50.

3

The Tylenol Crisis and Comeback Campaign: A Case Study in Corporate Social Responsibility

Anyone who doubts the importance of corporate image has only to read about the Johnson & Johnson Tylenol tragedy to become convinced. For decades, Johnson & Johnson enjoyed a popular public image until an unexpected tragedy struck which posed an immediate threat to the company's reputation. Only because of its concern for social responsibility and the resulting "reservoir of good will" was Johnson & Johnson able to deflect permanent damage to the company and its reputation.

REGAINING PUBLIC TRUST AND RESTORING THE JOHNSON & JOHNSON IMAGE

The tragedy statistics and recovery are remarkable when viewed from the human side of the story. Johnson & Johnson's willingness to accept responsibility for the tragedy and to communicate with Tylenol users guaranteed that the company image endured intact. Johnson & Johnson kept the public informed and reassured consumers with a message which came across loud and clear. That message was "Trust us." What made it work was its foundation in the company's forty-year-old credo. Every decision made in response to the Tylenol crisis rested in the corporate philosophy of doing business by putting "the interest of the consumer first."

Johnson & Johnson quickly disseminated accurate information to protect the company's reputation. Two factors proved central: being open and honest with the press, and responding immediately. Every decision was visible and demonstrated corporate responsibility.

Pointing to two or three critical considerations to ensure a credible corporate image, Corporate Vice President for Corporate Public Relations, Lawrence G. Foster, emphasized, "establishing a solid corporate reputation, and business philosophy are the basics. The public learns quicker about these if you have a group of competent professionals to communicate the company's good qualities to its various publics."[1]

Foster and members of his staff shared the Tylenol crisis story with public relations professionals across the nation. As guest speakers for the National Capitol Chapter, Public Relations Society of America, Foster recounted the tragedy and comeback in a vivid presentation. It is a success story without parallel in U.S. corporate history. Foster reported:

No crisis management plan would have been sufficient in the face of the Tylenol poisonings because not even the best of managers could have planned for a tragedy of that proportion. Fortunately, Johnson & Johnson had a 40-year-old corporate business philosophy to turn to. That philosophy established the company's priorities and defined its responsibilities to its constituencies. Although such a philosophy is not unique to Johnson & Johnson, it served us immeasurably in responding to and managing the greatest crisis ever to confront our business.

Johnson & Johnson's handling of the Tylenol crisis is a classic case of a corporation responding to public fears. Following the tragedy, the company launched a rescue which acknowledged public concern and took immediate remedial actions. But the foundation for the company's action had already been in place far earlier, giving the company a starting place to act promptly and with direction to minimize the adverse effects of the crisis. By avoiding the necessity of formulating an impromptu crisis-management philosophy to handle the situation, Johnson & Johnson preserved its positive corporate image.

LAYING THE GROUNDWORK FOR SOCIAL RESPONSIBILITY

In the mid-1940s, the late Robert Wood Johnson developed the then revolutionary business credo dealing with "corporate responsibility." A pioneer in business philosophy, Johnson wrote:

Institutions, both public and private, exist because the people want them, believe in them, or at least are willing to tolerate them. The day has passed when business was a private matter—if it ever really was. In a business society, every act of business has social consequences and may arouse public interest. Every time business hires, builds, sells or buys, it is acting for . . . people as well as for itself, and it must be prepared to accept full responsibility.

Tragedy Strikes

At the time he wrote about corporate responsibility in the 1940s, Johnson had no idea that his viewpoints would have such far-reaching implications in 1982, when an unknown criminal laced Tylenol capsules with cyanide, thus killing seven people in the Chicago area in one night.

The Chicago deaths touched off the biggest consumer product scare in history. Aside from the personal tragedies, Johnson & Johnson was thrown without warning into the incredible situation of coping with a crisis for which U.S. corporate history offered no precedent. Foster noted, "There is no crisis plan to cover an event of this scope. We learned, for the first time, a new form of terrorism, terrorism that strikes in the home."

How did Johnson & Johnson handle the crisis? Robert Wood Johnson had provided the groundwork for public trust by identifying a set of responsibilities which the company relied upon during the Tylenol tragedy. Equally important, this action was taken immediately after the crisis occurred. Johnson & Johnson management, because of its belief in and understanding of the corporate credo, knew precisely what had to be done to protect the public. It was crisis management at its best largely because the framework for the positive decisions made by Johnson & Johnson management to handle the crisis had been put in place decades earlier when the company was founded on sound and responsible philosophy.

The Johnson & Johnson Credo

David R. Clare, Johnson & Johnson president and executive committee chairman, commented, "Crisis planning did not see us through this tragedy nearly so much as the sound business management philosophy that is embodied in our credo. It was the credo that prompted the decisions that enabled us to make the right early decisions that eventually led to the comeback phase."

The credo Clare referred to, quoted in full here, is a simple, four-paragraph document written by Robert Wood Johnson. The credo reads:

Our Credo

We believe our first responsibility is to the doctors, nurses and patients, to mothers and all others who use our products and services. In meeting their needs everything we do must be of high quality. We must constantly strive to reduce our costs in order to maintain reasonable prices. Customers' orders must be serviced promptly and accurately. Our suppliers and distributors must have an opportunity to make a fair profit.

We are responsible to our employees, the men and women who work with us throughout the world. Everyone must be considered as an individual. We must respect their dignity and recognize their merit. They must have a sense of security in their jobs. Compensation must be fair and adequate, and working conditions clean, orderly and safe. Employees must feel free to make suggestions and complaints. There must be equal opportunity for employment, development and advancement for those qualified. We must provide competent management, and their actions must be just and ethical.

We are responsible to the communities in which we live and work and to the world community as well. We must be good citizens—support good works and charities and bear our fair share of taxes. We must encourage civic improvements and better health and education. We must maintain in good order the property we are privileged to use, protecting the environment and natural resources.

Our final responsibility is to our stockholders. Business must make a sound profit. We must experiment with new ideas. Research must be carried on, innovative programs developed and mistakes paid for. New equipment must be purchased, new facilities provided and new products launched. Reserves must be created to provide for adverse times. When we operate according to these principles, the stockholders should realize a fair return.

—Johnson & Johnson

According to James Burke, Johnson & Johnson's chairman and chief executive officer,

Two things are clear to us. The first is that the value system, as articulated in the credo, now permeates the company in a way that could not have been possible without the crisis. The credo was tested—and it worked. Further, we learned that the reputation of the corporation, which has been carefully built for over 90 years, provided a reservoir of good will among the public, the people in the regulatory agencies, and the media, which was of incalculable value in helping to restore the brand.

This attitude, a direct result of the credo which had produced the "reservoir of good will," helped Johnson & Johnson survive one of the worst tragedies in corporate history.

IMMEDIATE ACTIONS

After learning of the Chicago area poisonings on September 30, 1982, Johnson & Johnson management took immediate steps to inform the Food and Drug Administration. The company also recalled the product in thirty-one states, suspended all advertising of Tylenol, cleared Chicago area drugstores of the product, alerted the medical community by contacting them with 450,000 mailgrams, set up special telephone lines, and informed the media.

Initial events in the tragedy continued to unfold. The product recall uncovered seventy-five contaminated capsules in eight bottles. Thirty-one million bottles were destroyed, eight million were tested. Copycat crimes in late October complicated the tragedy as attempts to exploit the crime were repeated across the country. By early October, capsule production was halted completely and a $100,000 reward was posted. Throughout October additional steps were taken. The World Health Organization alerted suppliers around the world to protect overseas markets, and sixty-four government drug regulatory agencies became involved.

Johnson & Johnson employees were immediately informed and volunteer employees at McNeil Consumer Products Company, makers of Tylenol, were trained to handle calls from concerned consumers. Executive briefings were held periodically throughout the crisis.

Press queries, normally ranging from 700 to 800 per year, swelled to 2,000 in October alone. A press log was kept throughout the tragedy. Foster explained its use.

The press log, which was researched and updated for accuracy, included the name, title, news organization, phone number, address, etc., of every one of the 2,500 plus calls on the Tylenol story in the first several months, as well as everyone who wrote a by-line story, which we researched from the clips as they came in. It was used in numerous ways to commmunicate with the people closest to the story including inviting them to the video press conference (via satellite) which was our initial event in the Tylenol comeback. Some 600 reporters turned out, making it the largest press conference (I am told) ever held.

THE EXTENT OF ADVERSE EFFECTS CAUSED BY THE TRAGEDY

To understand how pervasive the tragedy had become, Johnson & Johnson hired the Compton Agency to perform a seven-week survey that included approximately 7,000 interviews. The findings showed that 90 percent of the population knew of the tragedy. And, importantly, a significant 90 percent of the population felt that Johnson & Johnson was not to blame and had acted in the public interest.

THE ROAD BACK

The recovery plan was launched in early November 1982, soon after the senseless tragedy occurred. A national sales relaunch meeting took place. The company mobilized 2,250 salespeople from its affiliate companies, and they made one million personal calls on all facets of the health delivery system that used or sold Tylenol, from physicians, nurses, and hospitals to drug and food outlets. On November 11, a video conference was made available to some 3,000 television stations across the country. In thirty cities some 600 reporters turned out to attend the press conference. During the press conference, toll-free numbers were flashed on the screen and 430,000 consumers called to ask for coupons to repurchase Tylenol. Approximately 80 million coupons worth $2.50 each were distributed through newspaper supplements. The company later produced a Tylenol Comeback Brochure summarizing all of these events for the news media.

An in-house video network was used extensively to keep employees informed. Five videotapes running an hour in length reached approximately 77,000 employees. According to Foster, "The videotapes covered every facet of the Tylenol tragedy and replayed for our employees many of the newscasts covering the story. In addition, we gave them a complete rundown on how we were dealing with the crisis internally."

Johnson & Johnson executives appeared on all the major television news magazines including *60 Minutes, Donahue, Today, Nightline, CBS Evening News*, and *The McNeill-Lehrer Report*. McNeil sales representatives made some seventy-five appearances on local television talk shows across the nation. The extent of television coverage of the tragedy was mind-boggling. In New York City alone, during the first week of the crisis, there were twelve hours of news coverage on television. The story became one of the most widely covered news events since the Vietnam War.

Results of the Recovery

The results of these efforts are shown clearly in the figures. Prior to the tragedy Tylenol was the most successful over-the-counter nonaspirin pain reliever on the market. Immediately following the poisonings, the future of Tylenol was understandably in grave doubt. But only five months later, Tylenol had recaptured 70 percent of its former market share. A year after the tragedy, the share climbed back to over 80 percent. In a *New York Times* article, Shearson/American Express estimates Tylenol now boasts an approximate 30 percent share of the $1.2 billion market for nonaspirin pain relievers, compared to the 37 percent share it had prior to the Chicago area deaths.[2]

In the same article, Stephen Greyser, professor of marketing at Harvard Business School, remarks, "It's been about as effective a rescue job as I've seen in Marketing."[3]

Robert Wood Johnson felt deeply that unless business recognized corporate responsibility, it could not be successful in the long run. He believed attention to corporate responsibility would be not only moral, but profitable as well. For nearly forty years, succeeding Johnson & Johnson managements have adhered to the same belief. And Johnson's convictions proved true. His credo of social responsibility proved beneficial, both morally and profitably, throughout the Tylenol crisis.

Johnson & Johnson employees strongly believe that the Tylenol tragedy reaffirms the wisdom of having a written philosophy. Despite the enormity of the Tylenol tragedy, the corporation's image as a social and cultural entity remains unblemished.

NOTES

1. Personal and written interview with Lawrence G. Foster, Corporate Vice President, Corporate Public Relations, Johnson & Johnson. A special word of gratitude to Mr. Foster for his valuable input into this work.

2. *New York Times*, September 17, 1983.

3. Ibid.

4

Atlantic Richfield Corporation: A Model Corporate Image Program

The Johnson & Johnson experience demonstrates how a strong, positive image gave the company the "reservoir of good will" necessary to see it through an unprecedented crisis. Unlike crisis management, however, oil companies have long endured a negative public image and have had to develop long-term image-building programs to reverse widely held public skepticism about "big oil." The public generally regards big oil companies as entirely profit-motivated—indifferent to the environment, to the needy who cannot pay high fuel bills in winter months, and even to the "energy crisis" facing all Americans. While Americans are forced to conserve energy through high fuel costs, the public perceives big oil companies as failing to invest their large profits in developing new energy technologies which will alleviate the nation's future energy problems.

MISTRUST AND CONFUSION ABOUT BIG OIL

Besides the negative "big oil" image during the early- to mid-1970s, the public has come to believe that oil companies keep fuel costs high. Recent oil gluts have, at times, appeared to confuse the public about the reality of an energy crisis. Though public confidence seems to have risen, some still view the crisis as an excuse on the part of oil companies to charge exorbitant prices. Others maintain that the seriousness of the energy crisis had been exaggerated. For others, energy no longer is a major concern. They want to forget the energy crisis and return to the good times of Sunday drives, motor vacations, big cars, and recreational vehicles.

On a recent trip to California I was forced, due to a flight cancellation, to land at Los Angeles International Airport during peak rush hours. Anyone who has had that experience knows traffic bottlenecks turn an ordinary one-hour car ride into several hours. A frequent observation by east coasters is the dependency west coasters have upon their automobiles. Those who live on the west coast give little thought to jumping into the car and driving for a couple of hours to keep an appointment. The compactness of Manhattan and the relative ease of a taxi or subway ride are soon forgotten. Experiencing rush-hour, mega-lane traffic creeping from suburb to suburb readily brought to mind how quickly we forgot the oil embargo of the early 1970s. How soon the quadrupled prices, long lines at the pumps, and downright hatred of the local gas station attendant have slipped our minds. In the end, the seesaw effect of shortage and abundance serves to erode oil industries' public credibility.

At the time of the oil embargoes, we directed our malice to big oil and the profit motive of big business. The public image of big oil suffered. The public hue and cry blamed the oil industry—damaging public trust that has not yet been repaired. It is against this backdrop of mistrust and confusion about the energy crisis (although the mid-1980s have seen an ease in public opinion) that large oil companies have had to form positive corporate images.

ATLANTIC RICHFIELD DEVELOPS IMAGE THROUGH COMMUNICATIONS

To reverse the persistent negative public opinion, Atlantic Richfield Company (ARCO) has taken great strides to realign its image. Through its corporate communication program which defined and conveyed a positive image, ARCO has rebuilt public confidence. The level of sophisticated know-how, as well as the dedication and enthusiasm displayed at ARCO, shaped and maintained a continuously emerging image that consumers and other publics trust.[1]

Because this far-reaching communication plan encompasses the lessons of this book, I will share with you highlights from ARCO's program. The lessons of ARCO's communication provide capsule guidelines from which any organization, large or small, can learn. Although ARCO is a giant, its program components directly address constituent needs.

The major factor behind ARCO's social sensitivity and action is its top executive leadership. CEO and President William F. Keischnick has had a clear vision of the constructive role a large business corporation and its executives should play in American society. His strong public speeches have been partial evidence of their concern. Just as important have been the many day-to-day actions which dramatize his commitment to social policies and programs.

Examples of ARCO's leadership in action abound. First, the company's top officers focused the executive committee's attention on the social and political environment, setting aside time for weekly discussion of important external developments. Second, they encouraged ARCO employees to become involved in community programs, and they stressed that this involvement is one criterion to determine promotions even among top executives. Third, top executives, amidst pressures to maximize profitability, have been expected to approve substantial expenditures for environmental control and community impact programs. Fourth, they have been expected to propose specific community-oriented programs and policies.

An effective management technique for encouraging compliance with social policies, these specific social performance objectives included monitoring the performance of executives and managers based on pre-set criteria. The company evaluates its topmost executives, including operating-company presidents, on their progress in affirmative action and on their personal community involvement. Although ARCO readily admits that setting social performance criteria is much less apparent below the topmost layer of management, ARCO executives agree that the performance objectives and monitoring policy ought to be encouraged at all management levels.

Communicating the company's continuing commitment to its social policies and to the social vision of its top officers has been one of ARCO's strong points. Company employee publications, particularly the *ArcoSpark*, regularly report company decisions regarding environmental control, community affairs, and employee relations.

Another major factor behind ARCO's public image has been its commitment to key issues formalized in corporate policy statements. For example, a "policy on relationships with employees" covers affirmative action, safe work environments, salaries and benefits, employee career development, open communications between employees and executives, and a corporate commitment to revise detailed policies in response to changing employee needs.

Management awareness of social issues has exemplified ARCO's willingness to define and communicate a credible corporate image. Though the current program is far-reaching, has specific objectives, is supported by top management, and has a sound monitoring system, ARCO is the first to admit that weaknesses exist. Nevertheless, in the energy industry's confrontation with the relatively new imperative of communication, ARCO can conservatively be said to have gained a tremendous headstart.

IDENTITY AND OTHER PROBLEMS

It is unlikely that anything as deep-rooted as the public's negative view of the oil industry will be reversed in a short time or with little effort. However, a company that prefers to enjoy continued public favor is well advised to communicate a distinct, differentiated image. Having made the transition from an "oil company" to a diversified energy/resources company and back to energy and away from diversification, ARCO has opened the door to asserting its individuality and to setting in place a new public image.

This is not to suggest that ARCO's performance appears flawless, that all questions about social responsibility have been resolved, or that no challenges remain. The oil industry as a whole fumbled a lifetime oppportunity in the gasoline-line crisis to improve its image at the point of contact with consumers. In an industry that spends billions on advertising and public relations, day-to-day communication with its constituents degenerated into dog-eared sheet-boards with illiterately scrawled legends like No Unleded. The need to define and communicate a corporate identity on a continuous basis remains an ongoing challenge. Recognizing this, ARCO has gone beyond many companies in demonstrating genuine social concern and promoting joint citizen/corporate involvement to deal with public concerns. At the same time, it has made a quantum jump ahead of many contemporaries in recognizing that the conventional format of corporate good works is not enough and that a prime imperative in today's world is communication. In initiating dialogues in various forms on a variety of current issues, ARCO has opened a pathway of exciting potentialities on which it and other organizations can expand.

ARCO has responded to the challenges faced by big business, especially by the growing energy industry. ARCO was cast as a big oil company in the minds of consumers, to whom environmental and energy issues far outweighed the central thrust of refining crude oil. ARCO, with its foundation in domestic crude oil and natural gas, became active in all phases of the petroleum energy business. Solar power has been among the interests included in ARCO's attempt to transform the earth's resources into today's marketplace as well as tomorrow's.

Toward the broad goal of meeting this challenge, ARCO established a far-reaching communication program that included employee involvement at all levels. Activities were as diverse as the traditional communications activities of major corporations—a speakers bureau, consumer programs, editorial services, and press relations. Additionally, ARCO directly addressed public concerns for social responsibility through publications for internal and external publics. Preeminent among these publications is a booklet titled *Consumerism in the Eighties*. This booklet shows the results of a national survey of "Attitudes Toward the Consumer Movement" conducted by Louis Harris and Associates.

During 1982 and 1983 ARCO also sponsored a series of conferences called *Partnerships: Public/Private*. The Philadelphia conference on public/private partnerships marked the first time a large and diverse group had been brought together to discuss private sector responses to public issues. City mayors and business executives from across the country gathered to discuss public concerns and the means by which private enterprise and the nation's cities can build partnerships to tap new resources to shape a more efficient, humane, and responsible society. The chief reason for establishing the conference was stated in its proceedings: "The most pressing need is for the country's private and public institutions to rise above their adversarial history. Successful partnerships depend on people who trust one another and work together."[2]

Syndicated columnist Neal R. Peirce, in an opening article "Exploring the Public/Private Frontier," supports this view, tying the need directly to the corporation. According to Peirce, "The corporation deludes itself if it believes it can be consequential unless it engages in truly significant public activities." Peirce feels that we stand at the threshold of an era in which a wide variety of competitive, alternative service entities will offer the essential competition to provide legitimate choice and to get the dominant systems to change their ways. A strong corporate role, to precipitate the more rapid dawning of that new day, may be an appropriate and necessary concern of corporate strategic planning.

The most ambitious effort to measure corporate social responsibility was reported in the ARCO publication *Participation*, an ongoing report in pursuit of "social" purposes. Justification lies in the introduction to *Participation III*, a statement put forth by former ARCO president and CEO Thorton F. Bradshaw (RCA chairman). The opening statement reinforced the attempt to position corporate responsibility with public expectations when it pointed out:

But acknowledging the overwhelming importance of society's expectations does not relieve corporate managers of the necessity of determining just how that social mandate can be met. And "managing" a corporation's social obligation is far from simple. The corporation is widely and correctly viewed as having responsibilities that transcend the marketplace. But what are they? Is a company concerned only with its own operations, its own products, its own employees, and problems and opportunities that exist only in the communities in which it functions?

In response, former chairman Bradshaw asserted:

In the end, all that can really be regarded as certain and unchanging is that a corporation in its day-to-day operations must be sensitive to the public interest. A socially accountable corporation must be a "thoughtful" institution, able to rise above immediate economic interests and to anticipate the impact of its actions on all individuals and groups, from shareholders to employees to customers to fellow breathers of the air and fellow sharers of the land. A successful business organization must possess a moral sense as well as an economic sense.

Start with the present strong demands for environmental safeguards, energy conservation, material recycling, and the fullest measure of health and safety protection for worker and consumer, advised Bradshaw. He further recommended innovations to give us substitutes for increasingly inadequate supplies of raw materials, of which energy is only one. Challenges to the corporation itself, particularly in matters of corporate governance and the move toward "democratizing" the workplace, can enlarge business enterprises and respond to the public's demand for deeper social involvement. But corporations must voluntarily meet the challenge or they will be coerced into it through increasing outside intervention in their internal affairs.

Present chief executive officer William F. Kieschnick continues the line of thought put forth by former chairman Bradshaw. Whatever the eventual outcome of these and other issues, it seems obvious that the modern corporation must understand its role in society and be able to account for it with much the same precision hitherto reserved for financial reporting.

THE PROGRAM

The following pages highlight ARCO's communication efforts with the many publics it serves. Among these publics are consumers, dealers, internal human resources, the community, minorities, the government, and all who share the growing concern for environmental protection and energy issues. These highlights exemplify how sound corporate communications build a credible corporate image.

Consumer Affairs

Safety. ARCO believes in promoting its economic role with care. Product quality and safety have always made good business sense. But these objectives demand more intense commitment as consumer and business awareness grows, scientific knowledge expands, and government regulations proliferate. This commitment places high value on information.

"Our perceptions have changed as to what we need to know," says Don Stieghan, corporate manager of toxicology and product safety. "We've become increasingly sensitive to the importance of describing the characteristics of our products—to our customers, as well as to our employees."

Several years ago ARCO voluntarily developed material safety data sheets for its products. These forms provided employees and customers concise information on safety and health hazards, handling and storage requirements, special precautions, and emergency procedures for individual products and particularly for petroleum and chemical products. A safety manager or representative kept tabs on the data sheets in the workplace, referring to them and making them available as needed.

Labeling, increasingly required by law, identifies and clarifies risks. Company labels, used most commonly on drums and cans of petroleum and chemical products, describe proper use of the product, spotlight dangers, and prescribe first aid and other emergency procedures.

Quality. Because product quality can be controlled and is not life-threatening, it presents a less thorny challenge than product safety. But consumers and ARCO put a heavy premium on both.

Manufacture of petroleum products provides a good example of the concern for quality control. Control starts with crude oil and moves on to process control at the refinery. Before leaving the refinery, products must be approved by a quality administration manager who operates independently of the refinery management. A quality assurance team in the field monitors the distribution system for adverse changes in product quality due to procedural errors.

At Anaconda Industries, a former ARCO affiliate, each plant and its departments used a numerical quality performance goal. Returned orders were analyzed and tallied according to both the material and value-added costs of the product. Once the staff determined which department was the cause of dissatisfaction, it assessed the costs against that department. The information appeared on a monthly Quality Performance Index report.

"This system enables us to measure customer satisfaction in dollars and aids in pinpointing problems" explained Rod Thorpe, director of metallurgy and research. The approach got results. In 1979 Anaconda Industries attained its highest level of customer satisfaction since it implemented the index in 1970, reducing the incidence of returns to .65 percent of its shipments.

In the Marketplace

The issue of price, of course, has special relevance to any discussion of an oil company's social responsibility. The questions must be asked frankly. Is ARCO or any other oil company acting responsibly by nearly doubling the wholesale price of its chief product, gasoline, in one year (1979)? In view of the inflationary effect of higher energy prices generally, is ARCO justified to argue, as it has, for the decontrol of domestic crude oil prices? What should the company's position be on energy prices and their impact on society?

Some of the answers to these questions, of course, lie in the fact that ARCO does not have a totally free hand in pricing. Much of the 1979 increase, in fact, was due to OPEC's doubling its crude oil price. In addition, an intricate set of federal rules and regulations governs price and distribution. This continues to hold the price of domestic crude oil below the world level.

ARCO's philosophy toward pricing, in short, maintains that pricing responsibility should encourage realism after years of national self-deception. Eventually, cheap, unlimited supplies of energy may again become available to Americans, perhaps through development of a replenishable source such as solar or nuclear fusion. Until that day comes, however, Americans must develop and conserve their precious supplies of oil, gas, and other conventional resources. And they must pay the price. Unfortunately, there is no alternative to this hard truth.

Dealing with Dealers

ARCO service station dealers are the most immediate link between the company and the consuming public. Independent business people operate nearly all the 8,300 stations selling the ARCO brand, making the area of dealer relations an important and sometimes delicate one.

The many changes triggered by the Arab oil embargo of 1973–1974 strained relations between the company and its dealers. Although tensions have eased, "the embargo changed the retail station dramatically," recalled Scott Stanworth, former manager of sales development for ARCO Petroleum Products Company. "Prices skyrocketed, supplies were short, stations couldn't stay open, service deteriorated. The public was angry and vented its frustration on the dealer."

As supplies normalized and the company once again had a product to sell, dealers were encouraged to return to their former level of service. "We initiated an aggressive educational program encouraging two-way communications between the company and the dealers and urging dealers to treat customers fairly. The situation has improved greatly as a result," noted Stanworth.

The company named its first dealer ombudsman in 1975, charging him with mediating dealer disputes or complaints that could not be satisfied through usual channels. However, through continuing personal contact and communication, the company attempted to unsnarl problems before they required ombudsman intervention. Dealer-training programs, for example, provided a week of instruction on up-to-date marketing, service and mechanic techniques, and working with the public.

Dealer representatives, who called regularly on clients, reinforced the training and helped problem solving. Regular publications promoted the communication process. In addition, dealer panels in various marketing regions furnished a forum for dealers and management to share views and vent grievances.

Listening to Customers

By responding to consumer inquiries and complaints quickly and courteously, ARCO achieves a high level of customer satisfaction, a particularly demanding task in today's business climate.

Arco Petroleum Products staffed a Customer Relations Department to handle complaints and inquiries and to initiate programs to promote customer satisfaction. The ARCO staff responded to approximately 6,500 general questions and complaints annually. "We try to handle all of these on a personal level," explained John Alexander, head of the department. "We may not always succeed, but our goal is to turn around a bad situation and keep the customer."

To achieve this, the staff acknowledged every call or letter within twenty-four hours, though it sometimes took longer to get an answer or solve a problem. If the complaint involved dealers, the staff arbitrated through the local sales office by contacting the dealers and urging them to resolve the difficulty.

Keeping Consumers Informed

Besides handling consumer complaints, ARCO makes a concerted effort to develop and disseminate objective and useful consumer information about products and energy issues.

The company prepares and distributes written and audiovisual materials to consumers. Distribution includes mailing literature, placing literature in service stations, and sponsoring public gatherings where consumer discussions take place. Topics such as octane rating, self-service, car care, energy conservation, and metric conversion are included in ARCO's efforts to inform consumers.

The company's Consumer Affairs Department, part of Public Affairs, spearheads continuing two-way communication with consumer advocates and other public interest groups. One of its prime responsibilities is to inform management about current and emerging issues and involve them directly in public interests.

In the past, the department arranged periodic "DIALOG" sessions between ARCO senior management and public interest group leaders. "DIALOG" was designed to short-circuit misunderstanding and rhetoric, while providing an effective format for dealing with public concerns. Initially, mistrust on all sides existed, but the company found that a candid, people-to-people discussion reduced suspicion and eased apprehensions.

Consumer Affairs has also presented a series of Contemporary Consumer Issues programs to give educators an opportunity to consider economic and social issues from the perspective of business, government, academic, and public interest advocates.

MOVING UP: INTERNAL HUMAN RESOURCES MANAGEMENT

Atlantic Richfield regards its 47,000 employees as a valuable asset. "Our employees represent one of our single most important resources for the future," stated former board chairman Anderson. "They are an integral component in the long-term strategy of our company, as vital to our success as the operating assets, financial capital, and confidence stockholders entrust to us."

The company trains supervisors at all levels to understand and respond to the differing needs of their staffs. ARCO actively promotes an employment policy based on fair and equal treatment of all, regardless of sex, age, race, or ethnic background. ARCO readily admits that top line managers are predominantly white males, but is quick to point out that these managers have worked for up to twenty-five years.

ARCO encourages and subsidizes employee efforts to improve skills and earn promotions. With Atlantic Richfield Replacement System, all ARCO companies list openings in *ArcoSpark*, the company newsletter. Listings attract more that 50,000 applicants annually. Of the 1,750 jobs listed each year, employees fill 60 percent.

Each ARCO company has its own training organization, with instruction ranging from how to operate a forklift to how to manage a company. To speed the process of promoting from within, special programs such as the management internship program started by ARCO Pipe Line Company have been implemented. Professionals and managers receive training in areas such as dealing with others, problem solving and public speaking. Furthermore, ARCO has helped employees pay for outside classes and has reimbursed up to 80 percent of tuition, books, and expenses for approved courses, as long as a return for the company is identified.

Since 1978, the active recruitment of women and a scholarship program for women have brought more of them into the ARCO tanker fleet. In fact, ARCO has ranked as a leader among oil companies in its percentage of female fleet personnel, with thirty-five women on sea duty, nine of them officers. Moreover, ARCO companies promote equal opportunities with dozens of smaller programs such as minority summer hires, internships, scholarships, and support of organizations helping minority groups.

On the international level, an agreement with the Indonesian government for oil production in the Java Sea resulted in the company's hiring and training many Indonesian citizens. By the end of 1979 ARCO had spent about $2.5 million on Indonesian employee training, and the company is presently training Indonesians for advancement.

Staying Well

Because employee health affects job performance, ARCO has expanded its role to help employees stay well. As part of this effort, Dr. Ron Schwartz, associate corporate medical director, communicates health and safety tips by writing a column on health issues for *ArcoSpark*. Topics include smoking, obesity, excessive sun exposure, and stress. The company has conducted monthly health seminars. Free emergency medical services are offered at locations with medical facilities and periodic medical checkups are provided for middle and top management.

ARCO employee relations policies treat alcoholism and drug abuse as illnesses which interfere with work and require treatment. Supervisors are trained to spot absence patterns and poor work performance that indicate a problem. Employees are referred, on a voluntary basis, to the Employee Assistance Program for help with drug or alcohol addiction, or other crises such as family or financial problems.

Looking out for Alumni

Retired employees have received a number of unusual benefits beyond an ample pension. Retirees and eligible dependents may continue in the company's group medical insurance plan until reaching Medicare age, when a group Medicare supplement plan takes over.

Retired workers have been occasionally rehired for special programs. In one such program, "Drive for Conservation," the company hired six retirees to staff the program's caravans, which toured the country teaching energy-saving habits to the public.

Keeping in Touch

The company operates a vast communication system to meet special needs. Published weekly, *ArcoSpark* carries news, features, and items of interest for the entire company. Telephone information systems allow employees to ask questions about policies and practices. Questions and answers are printed and distributed. And many operating companies and plants sponsor workplace meetings enabling employees and senior management to share views.

When Employees Move: A Special Concern

Most companies view moving as a necessary sacrifice to achieve career advancement. But concern for the costs of buying and selling homes, moving costs, and the rise of the two-career family have changed this attitude. Consequently, businesses now have more trouble than in the past finding people willing to accept transfers. As a result, companies must be increasingly responsive to the needs of employees and their families in planning relocations.

A prime example of sensitivity to this issue occurred when ARCO Coal Company moved its headquarters from Los Angeles to Denver. ARCO provided moving consultants and information about Denver as well as making allowances and loans to help employees buy new homes. At final count, about 75 percent of ARCO Coal's 131 Los Angeles employees accepted transfers. Those who remained were aided in finding other jobs.

OCCUPATIONAL SAFETY AND ENVIRONMENTAL PROTECTION

Due to the nature of its business, Atlantic Richfield adheres to a strict set of occupational and environmental safety standards. This is a special area not peculiar to most businesses, but ARCO's efforts, a part of the total communication program, go a long way toward promoting a positive corporate image regarding occupational safety and environmental issues.

One manager of corporate occupational and environmental protection noted that senior management—from the chairman and president down—expected everyone in the corporation to live up to the highest standards in this regard. He added, "Management values the environment and the individual. The company also wants to avoid the public distaste, if not hostility, generated by environmental, health, and safety disasters."

ARCO operating companies reinforce this long-standing commitment. "Each operating company—through its own management structure—stands accountable for carrying out its particular environmental, health, and safety responsibilities," emphasized Dr. Owen Thomas, manager of occupational and environmental protection for ARCO Petroleum. "The magnitude of prevailing and emerging regulations demands a high degree of accountability. We must answer not only to ourselves and our companies, but to the larger society. And we're willing to devote whatever resources it takes to honor our commitment."

Line managers, who account for performance in occupational and environmental protection, claim they are able to put "teeth" into mandated and voluntary programs because of the company's willingness to back its commitment with dollars. The company, in fact, regards such expenses as a legitimate cost of doing business.

The rapidly growing need for information has spurred a number of safety and environmental actions at ARCO. The company developed a sophisticated computerized system that records and makes available current health and safety data on products, workers, and workplace situations. Known as The Occupational Environmental Health Information System (TOEHIS), the system offers a comprehensive, cost-effective approach to meeting government reporting requirements and strengthening the company's overall environmental, health, and safety efforts.

Moreover, ARCO established a corporate-wide Occupational and Environmental Protection Council to deal more effectively with an increasingly complex regulatory climate. The Protection Council, headed by vice presidents from the operating companies, considered a variety of policies, programs, and communication efforts to promote corporate-wide consistency and compliance with related laws such as the Toxic Substances Control Act. ARCO also established a company-wide task force to develop procedures for employees to report "substantial risk" to health or the environment from suspect substances in the workplace.

The company established an innovative Environmental and Safety/Health Review Program that assessed how well major operating facilities follow the company's environmental protection policy and handle related issues. Each on-site review team consisted of three or four middle-management "peers" (usually engineering and operating managers and supervisors) from various departments within the operating companies. William Kelly, former corporate environmental services manager, noted, "We find they take back a new awareness and sensitivity to their own operations, so sometimes it's not only the plant being reviewed that implements changes."

Innovative Programs for Protecting the Environment

ARCO encounters numerous environmental problems due to the nature of its diversified business interests. Examples of innovative ARCO programs for correcting environmental disturbances are plentiful. Surface mining, for example, is a major environmental issue. As far back as 1975 the former ARCO Coal Company, now called ARCO Minerals, determined to find the best seed mixtures for trees and shrubs needed to revegetate and reclaim land it would mine in the Wyoming grasslands. As a result, replanting was begun at ARCO's Black Thunder mine in Wyoming's Powder River Basin.

The operating plan further demanded that land disturbances be kept to a minimum. Therefore, only about 160 acres were mined at one time. As the mine front advanced, the overburden, a layer of sand, clay, and rock, was replaced and contoured and then covered with topsoil. As a result, only one-fifth of the property, including plant site and revegetation areas, was in a state of disruption at any time.

The safe movement of crude oil has become especially important with the development of the Alaskan fields. ARCO Transportation freely admits there is no fail-safe protection from oil spilled at sea. But the company believes it has lowered the risks significantly through an expensive program to upgrade its tankers.

ARCO Transportation has spent more than $2 million in recent years to advance the safety of each of its tankers. A major chunk of this money went into installing inert gas systems, designed to prevent explosion or fire by maintaining low oxygen levels in the cargo tanks. The last of ARCO's company-owned fleet has been retrofitted with such a system, well in advance of the federal law that now requires all American tankers to install the system.

Innovative Occupational Safety Programs

Innovative industrial hygiene programs, such as its new Assess and Control Exposure (ACE) effort, gave ARCO an edge in protecting the health and safety of its employees. ACE offered a highly disciplined approach to identifying all chemicals and physical agents within each workplace, evaluating the degree of employee exposure to them, and initiating appropriate controls. In fact, ACE's scope exceeded the record-keeping and reporting requirements of various regulations.

ARCO Petroleum's handling of four refineries, where flash fires rank as a chief safety concern, exemplifies the company's concern for worker safety. Well aware of the danger, the company introduced an expensive protective clothing program, providing flame-resistant Nomex coveralls to refinery personnel. These coveralls saved four workers at the Philadelphia facility from severe injuries. But even before Nomex came on the scene, ARCO Petroleum's safety record had improved to one of the best in the country. The record is due, in large measure, to extensive safety programs, safety drills, meetings, incentives, and total managerial involvement.

ENERGY CONSERVATION

Atlantic Richfield's concern for energy began in the late 1960s when the then President Bradshaw warned that America was on the verge of running out of oil. ARCO quickly launched a far-reaching and highly successful campaign to improve energy efficiency in all its operations. When a second major oil crisis hit the country in 1978–1979 with the Iranian cutoff, public fears about supplies and prices mounted. ARCO decided the time was ripe to carry a strong conservation message into the community. Subsequently, ARCO's leadership in conservation has gained national recognition.

A first part of the two-pronged conservation effort began within its own operations. From 1972 to 1979, for example, ARCO Chemical Company saw a 36.8 percent improvement in energy conservation over its base figure. Several factors play a part in the conservation success story: educational programs, quarterly energy audits, maintenance improvements, operational controls and surveillance, revamping of manufacturing processes and equipment, restructuring of facilities, and ongoing commitment.

An example of these internal measures to conserve energy is evidenced at ARCO Chemical Company. Chuck Hudson, manager of ARCO Chemical Company's Lyondell complex at Channelview, Texas, credited the "total commitment" of the approximately 800 employees at the complex. Hudson further credited a new-employee orientation program and the installation of a steam line for the 37 percent reduction in Lyondell's energy consumption rate.

But internal efforts were only the first part of the two-pronged effort to conserve. The second effort was directed at spreading the word to the broader community. Because U.S. automobiles consume about one-half the oil burned in this country, an ARCO program aimed at America's drivers instilled an awareness of the importance of conservation.

Following the gasoline shortage in 1979, the company introduced its "Drive for Conservation" program. This public service taught motorists how to save gasoline by developing fuel-saving driving habits and paying attention to automobile maintenance. As a corollary to the "Drive," training kits were sent on request to high-school driver education teachers for classroom use. More than one million students were expected to use these instructional materials during the first year's circulation. More than 238,000 copies of a companion booklet, "Road to Conservation," were distributed to government officials, civic leaders, fleet transportation managers, educators, and others.

These programs are significant because they demonstrate "that a national training program can work, that Americans can, indeed, be educated to use less gas," suggests William Duke, manager of national programs.

ARCO's national advertising campaign in 1979–1980 also zeroed in on energy conservation, giving strong support to the "Drive" caravans. Since 1973 the company has spent the bulk of its advertising dollar to encourage public involvement in energy and other issues. The company's 1979 campaign used network television spots for the first time to advise Americans to go on an "energy diet." In addition, gasoline-saving tips were sent to motorists upon request. In 1980 the campaign appealed to the public's conscience and pocketbook with the theme "Conservation: It's the thing to do." The message, carried mainly in magazines and on television, was expected to reach 140 million Americans.

As part of its stepped-up conservation activities, ARCO expanded its innovative "Car Care: Not for Men Only" program to additional locations. The clinic employed hands-on demonstrations to teach motorists how to perform routine car checks and maintenance to improve gasoline mileage.

Denver was one of the most recent cities to benefit from ARCO's enthusiasm for ride sharing. With the cooperation of the Denver Chamber of Commerce, public relations representative Harold Craige put together a van pool workshop for organizations interested in starting ride-sharing programs.

Using what he termed a "shirt sleeve, nuts and bolts approach," Craige conducted more than thirty seminars for various companies and consulted with 150 businesses to establish third-party programs. At its peak, the program included more than 100 vans carrying commuters. At one time or another, up to 65 percent of Atlantic Richfield's work force in downtown Denver participated in some form of ride sharing, including van pooling.

In addition, since 1975 Atlantic Richfield Foundation has awarded $100,000 in support of transportation seminars in Los Angeles, Seattle, Philadelphia, Dallas, and Houston, giving some 200 government officials, transportation professionals, and college professors an opportunity to explore solutions to transportation problems.

COMMMUNITY AFFAIRS

ARCO takes its role as a corporate citizen seriously, especially in communities where it operates. The company believes a successful business must respond to a community's evolving needs. As an economic enterprise, ARCO recognizes its limits in promoting social change. Nevertheless, the company accepts responsibility for improving the quality of life.

ARCO's efforts to enhance community life cover a broad range of human needs and interests. They reflect more than a commitment of corporate funds. They also reflect understanding of the need to develop human resources. Consequently, volunteer programs and cooperative ingenuity play a vital role in the company's community involvement. Local, national, and international programs highlighted here give a sampling of ARCO's endeavors toward upgrading American life.

Building Better Communities

ARCO's active community involvement demonstrates the company's concern for direct social responsibility to improve the corporate image where it counts, where people see direct results.

Numerous examples include the work of ARCO Chemical Company, headquartered in Philadelphia, where ARCO Chemical rehabilitates deteriorating inner-city neighborhoods.

In Los Angeles the company opened The Center for Visual Art that showcases the work of contemporary artists. The gallery charges no admission and draws a broad audience of approximately 70,000 people annually.

In addition, ARCO has been one of the nation's largest corporate underwriters of public television, supporting many hours of quality educational and entertainment shows for family viewing. In 1984 ARCO put a sizable sum into sponsoring the Olympic games. The company supports fund-raising drives for local public television in many cities. In Denver, for instance, affiliated corporate organizations each contributed $1,500 to sponsor a telephone bank for one evening.

Through its involvement in Los Angeles's Plaza de la Raza, ARCO reaches an increasingly important segment of the population—the Hispanics—who until recently have been almost invisible to corporate America. Plaza de la Raza, which means "place of the people," is a bustling community center in the city's heavily Hispanic east side. The Plaza is the scene of instructional classes, cultural events, and community meetings.

But ARCO recognizes that money isn't the only answer to community needs. ARCO volunteers have been solid supporters of blood banks in many communities. In Lafayette, Louisiana, for example, 25 percent of ARCO Oil and Gas Company employees donated blood in local drives.

Recognizing that a simple idea can sometimes accomplish a great deal, ARCO donated thousands of seedlings in a program called "Growing Concern." Volunteers, including school children and other community members, planted trees to beautify parks, schools, public buildings, and residential areas.

Working with Youths

Atlantic Richfield further supports American youth activities, including a variety of national and local programs to promote education, self-esteem, and opportunities. The ARCO Jesse Owens Games, founded in 1965, are perhaps the premier example of the company's involvement with youths. The games sponsor preliminary meets in 250 counties and towns as well as fourteen regional events and the annual national championship held in Los Angeles.

The company sponsors Junior Achievement to acquaint young people with the virtues of private enterprise. During the school year, a group of young Junior Achievement members form a company, manufacture a product, and market it. They return profits and the original investment to their shareholders when the company liquidates at the semester's end.

ARCO and employee volunteers support programs at several predominantly minority schools in Dallas, Los Angeles, and Philadelphia. In Los Angeles, approximately 150 employees serve about 750 youngsters at two inner-city schools under the Joint Education Project.

In Philadelphia, ARCO Chemical supports PRIME (Philadelphia Regional Introduction to Minorities in Engineering), which prepares minority junior and senior high school students for engineering careers. Atlantic Richfield Foundation donated $50,000 to PRIME in 1980 alone. The program's positive results show that about 75 percent of involved students attend engineering school or pursue related careers.

Another effort is aimed at reaching young people in trouble with the law. ARCO Petroleum began an experimental program at the ARCO Dealer Training Center in El Monte, California. It enrolled four teenagers in four weeks of job-training courses and in the same intensive, one-week auto tune-up course offered ARCO station managers. The program ended successfully for the pilot group. Two youths found jobs, one began a paid auto mechanics apprenticeship, and the fourth signed up for more instruction. The training has since been streamlined and expanded to include more disadvantaged youth.

Encouraging Volunteerism

ARCO policy encourages employees to become involved in politics and government, charity work, and other civic and community activities. Employees have been able to spend a limited amount of paid company time performing volunteer work for company-sponsored programs, such as Junior Achievement activities. Beyond hours paid by the company, many volunteer their own time. Volunteering is one form of direct employee involvement with local communities that strengthens the corporate/community bond and helps cement a concerned corporate image.

Sharing management expertise with community groups reinforces this bond. ARCO Oil and Gas Company, for instance, loaned an executive to the Bakersfield, California, United Way on a half-time basis for about six weeks. The company contributed a substantial portion of this valuable employee's time because it recognized the fund's importance to the community.

Boosting Minority Businesses

The company has established a Minority Business Development Program to promote accountability and success in helping qualified minority suppliers and contractors join the economic mainstream. Through the program, the company voluntarily set a yearly goal to increase its business with minority vendors. To qualify, a business must present proof of ownership by a Black, Hispanic, Asian, Indian, or native Alaskan.

ARCO has employed two full-time professionals to work with minority firms, giving technical and other assistance. The company also works with government and private programs that aid minority businesses. In addition, it has published a directory of qualified minority businesses to guide buyers.

The company's Minority Bank Deposit Program promotes the economic growth of those who have been denied opportunity in the past. ARCO has deposited $40,000 cash in each of the 65 minority and female-owned financial institutions now involved in the program. To qualify, a bank or savings and loan association must prove female or minority ownership, be financially viable, and be involved in helping the community.

Locating and Developing New Communities

Prior to implementing major corporate changes that affect communities in which the company is located, ARCO studies the socioeconomic impact that its new or modified operating facilities will have on the community. Especially in sparsely populated rural areas, the company does everything possible to mitigate any negative effects.

Sometimes a company requires facilities that could, in theory, be built almost anywhere. ARCO goes beyond looking for reasonably priced land in a suitable area. According to Jean Moore, manager of major office projects, "We also want to find a location where we'll be able to maintain or even improve the level of minority and women employees." Moore continues, "We make an effort to find a location where we will be able to use energy-saving employee transportation and minority vendors. We also look for a location that will offer a good quality of life for employees who will be transferred there."

INVESTING ABROAD

Company operations in foreign countries center on finding and developing mineral resources that are scarce or nonexistent at home. But just as the company looks beyond the obvious in locating facilities in this country, it evaluates foreign locations on criteria beyond resource potential. ARCO's political and economic analysts assess the stability of a country's leadership and the basis of its support, the income level of the population, the economic situation in terms of inflation and other factors, and the country's relationship with its neighbors.

In a question-answer session, former ARCO chairman Anderson stated it best when he said, "We feel that anything that creates job opportunities in countries that have extensive unemployment is making a social contribution."

PHILANTHROPY

Atlantic Richfield views philanthropy as more than a random dispensing of corporate wealth in support of charitable activities. Beyond the obvious humanitarian benefits, corporate philanthropy focuses on improving the quality of life and promoting the pluralism that gives American society its strength.

Atlantic Richfield Foundation operates as the company's chief philanthropic arm. Established in 1963, the Foundation is a private, tax-exempt organization funded solely by ARCO.

Foundation grants, enumerated in an annual report, have been awarded to nonprofit tax-exempt public charities in one of seven categories including:

1. Institutions of higher education, particularly independent colleges and universities.
2. Programs in the arts and humanities, with emphasis on bringing cultural experiences to segments of society not presently enjoying them.
3. Nonprofit community service organizations whose programs and activities seek to strengthen the sense of community.
4. Selected national health-care programs and occasional hospital capital projects.
5. Environmental programs, including natural land preservation, wildlife conservation, research, and educational efforts.
6. United funds providing accessible and appropriate social services to meet human needs of diverse communities.
7. Public information and miscellaneous programs of national organizations that address important domestic and international public policy issues.

PUBLIC POLICY ADVOCACY AND GOVERNMENT RELATIONS

Management at ARCO realizes that in a complex society government regulations and the resulting costs are here to stay. Yet the company is unwilling to abdicate its role in shaping public policy. At the risk of occasional consumer disapproval and disapproval from business leaders and others, ARCO continues to speak out on issues of public interest, particularly those affecting the energy industry.

Consequently, the company has gained a reputation as a maverick among the major energy companies. While ARCO separates itself from the pack, it does not do so just to be different. The company follows a carefully charted course that constantly seeks to reconcile the public interest with the profit motive, to ensure that government and business continue to coexist peacefully.

The company's political perspective differs in other instances from industry positions, although ARCO does try to gain consensus on issues through participation in trade associations. For example, as far back as 1971 when most oil companies opposed the idea, ARCO endorsed the use of federal highway funds for mass transit.

ARCO has also supported comprehensive oil-spill legislation. In fact, the company affirmed the need for remedial legislation in the case of inactive waste sites. Recognizing political realities, the company has actively offered constructive legislative alternatives to the extremely broad hazardous substances release coverage, stressing more equitable liability provisions and ways of financing emergency response funds.

The company's Public Affairs Department works daily with governmental agencies on proposed legislation. A team of twelve registered Washington lobbyists and seventeen others dealing with state governments in offices located throughout the country provide information for elected officials and their staffs about how specific measures affect ARCO. They communicate the company's point of view to officials and lend an ear to the government's side as well. Company executives frequently testify at Congressional hearings.

Responsibility for helping company representatives sort legislation and speak with one voice falls to the Planning and Government Analysis Section. Its professional staff studies and tracks legislation in issue clusters and leads in developing company white papers on pertinent topics such as public lands policy, national health care, and hazardous and toxic substances. It also serves the operating companies and lobbyists by keeping them informed about pending legislation and government actions.

Involving Employees in Politics

Employees constitute one of the company's most effective communications techniques. Surprisingly, post-Watergate election reform laws have promoted greater employee involvement in the political process. Since 1975, thousands of ARCO men and women have joined the Civic Action Program (CAP), a voluntary, nonpartisan organization that educates employees about the issues and encourages them to participate in shaping public policies that affect them as private citizens.

A full-time CAP staff of eight plans more than 280 events each year and issues periodic publications such as CAP Reports. But the group itself never takes a stand on the issues. Instead, it operates to inform employees and stimulate involvement in local, state, or national politics.

A model for other companies, CAP offers a mechanism for employees to meet legislators face-to-face through lunchtime programs at company facilities, candidate coffees and dinners in private homes, and even group visits to state capitols. For many, talking to their representative on a person-to-person basis is a new and memorable experience.

Employees also give financial support to candidates of their choice through the Concerned Citizens Fund. Political reform legislation paved the way for such corporate-sponsored political action committees, similar to those of organized labor. Unlike many political action committees, ARCO's Concerned Citizens Fund allows participants to select candidates to receive their donations, or they may turn that selection over to the Fund's Contributions Committee. Naturally, participation in the Fund remains both voluntary and confidential.

With the growth of government and regulations, company involvement with the political process is bound to continue expanding. "I really believe that we have to get involved," former chairman Anderson explained. "It's not a matter of choice. . . . In the past, the corporate world was aloof from political problems. But, as we begin to see what's going on, we see that democratic societies are in trouble—and it's time we were heard from."

ARCO'S IMAGE: LESSONS IN COMMUNICATIONS

While up against the odds of reversing the public's negative view of "big oil," ARCO has made considerable strides toward improving public perception of the company's name. ARCO has achieved its improved image primarily through aggressive communications and through demonstration of community involvement ranging from good deeds for the disadvantaged to entering the political arena.

Fortunately, most corporations do not begin with a negative image. Nevertheless, ARCO has taken positive steps to build an image—practical steps which corporate managers should consider and can implement to improve or create image. Obviously, ARCO views communications and public works as two key factors in the image-building process.

NOTES

1. Written interview and materials supplied by Henry E. Spier, Consultant, Executive Communications; Myrna Plost, Director, Education Programs; and Judy Baird, Government Relations Representative. A special word of gratitude to them for sharing their thoughts and materials for use in this work.

2. *Partnerships: Public/Private*, Conference Report (Los Angeles: Editorial and Design Services, March 29–31, 1982).

PART II

The Corporate Image Program

5

Up Front: What the Public Sees

In a recent episode of the top-rated television soap *Dynasty*, antagonist Alexis Colby explains that the success image of the make-believe Denver-Carrington Oil Company must be upheld at all costs. To secure top ratings, *Dynasty* producers carefully design the program's elaborate business sets. Wall-to-wall carpeting, futuristic ivory and glass desks, designer seating, and fully equipped wet bars fill the offices of the towering glass skyscrapers. And high-tech meeting rooms with mahogany walls and massive conference tables reflect power and success.

Dynasty, although a television series, affords a lesson in real-world corporate image perception. Viewer surveys reveal that the audience relates to the high-powered corporate success image portrayed. Exterior symbols appeal to viewers and convey the corporate image of financial success.

Exterior symbols are a first indication of the stature of a business. The corporate name, logo, building address, office layout, furnishings, company cars, service vehicles, stationery, and product labels are among many outward visuals that carry the corporate image to the outside world. These symbols trigger conscious and subconscious images in the public mind. Examples from reality rather than the world of television include New York's Rockefeller Plaza, which signals success in the financial world. And Chicago's Sears Tower soars skyward as proof of an American rags-to-riches story of what began as a humble mail-order business that mushroomed into a multibillion dollar corporation.

ECONOMIC IMPACT

For the new or expanding company, exterior image is not simply a visual symbol of success but represents public recognition of product quality, and it goes without saying that this figures into the profit margin. For example, after a host of financial difficulties in the mid-1970s, Consolidated Edison (Con Ed) of New York is now in sound financial shape. The turnaround can be partially attributed to the corporation's exterior identity remake. Charles Luce, former chairman and chief executive officer, sought the services of a number of graphic designers, industrial designers, and architects to overhaul Con Ed's slipping visual image. These professionals developed corporate colors, revamped slogans and printed materials, and altered the company's fleet of service vehicles to meet modern design standards.

Exterior portrayal is a serious building block in the corporate image-building plan. Identity consultant Dennis Moran feels strongly about the need for corporate image and for managements having a say in defining and communicating that image. In "Corporate ID Is Your Major Resource" Moran stresses, "An identity consultant can help management understand that varied identity elements are similar to tangible assets and should be managed and controlled as such."[1]

MAKING THE CHANGE: THE MERGER OF SOVRAN FINANCIAL CORPORATION

A growing number of companies are deciding that their images are too confining, misleading, or simply do not reflect the dynamism of their business. Now, more than ever, a company changes its identity to accompany either industry diversification or specialization—strengthening and distinguishing its identity. Many forces come together to reshape the structure and images of industry and the companies within those industries. Perhaps the most obvious recent example is that of the divestiture of American Telephone & Telegraph.

Another significant industry facing forced restructure is banking. Deregulation of the banking industry, resulting in growth of new services and markets, is a prime example of an industry undergoing an identity crisis and doing something about it. Financial institutions represent one of the largest groups who have been changing names and images in recent years.

Pat Allen, financial observer and writer, reports, "In an effort to take advantage of financial services deregulation, many savings institutions are using name and charter changes to become stronger forces in the market place." She goes on to say:

The most common charter conversion is that from a savings association to a savings bank, and 11 state mutual savings banks have converted to federal charters.

Lack of public confidence in savings associations has been yet another impetus for change. Finally, many institutions have perceived a need to move from geographically limited identities.[2]

Sovran Financial Corporation, headquartered in Norfolk, Virginia, offers a prime example of demonstrating steps that must be taken when undergoing a complete corporate image change. Because the recent corporate image make-over undergone by Sovran typifies the struggles an organization faces and the solutions it can achieve, aspects of the image remake are presented here as an example from which business leaders can draw.

The corporate image revamp happened as a result of the December 30, 1983, consummation of the merger of Virginia National Bankshares, Inc., and First & Merchants Corporation as well as their subsidiary banks, Virginia National Bank and First & Merchants National Bank. Forces behind the merger and restructuring were cited in a speech by Sovran's chairman of the board and chief executive officer, C. A. Cutchins, III. Cutchins pointed first to the diminishing role of state boundaries as a barrier to competition. Second, rapid innovation in communications and data-processing technologies is producing dramatic changes in the form of and accessibility to financial products. This innovation costs money and requires a commitment of resources beyond the capacity of many small- and medium-sized banks. The third major force at work, and perhaps the most serious, is the decreasing net interest margins which result from deregulation. Smaller spreads between the cost of acquiring funds and the price at which they are loaned decrease profitability and investment resources. This in turn reduces the ability to fund opportunities that would offset the eroding margins.[3] These three factors clearly suggest that continued success required a more meaningful market position and a greater availability of resources.

Attention to Name Selection: Sovran Bank, N.A.

Sovran Bank's name change reflects the careful attention given to the procedures in selecting a new name. After a review of 8,000 names submitted by employees of both banks involved in the mergers, the name Sovran was selected. Final name selection was aided by Glenn Monigle and Associates, Denver consultants for marketing communications and corporate design. Sovran feels extraordinarily confident about the new name because it so well meets the criteria established at the outset for choosing a name. Those criteria include:

1. The word *Virginia* could not be used because four of the seven major banks in the state include the name *Virginia*. This causes confusion to the public and out-of-state investors and security analysts.

2. The new name should suggest leadership, stature, strength, dignity, seriousness of purpose, and "service orientation dedicated to high quality."

3. The name should be functional and distinctive. It should also be easy to remember, geographically inclusive, brief, and phonetic.

The name *Sovran* meets other criteria. Besides being short, memorable, and strong, it could be accommodated by an eye-catching design that quickly met with employee, customer, and public approval and acceptance.

Overall, the name *Sovran* brings to mind an image of reliability. The selection of a name for the new holding company and bank was an important step forward in the complex process of merging the two corporations, particularly since that name had to recognize much more than the physical creation of a new institution.

Management was looking for a name that would indicate leadership, strength and stature, and commitment to service. They also wanted a name that would represent a fresh outlook, a progressive new system that maintained the two banks' traditional values and standards, yet was distinctive and represented a departure from anything the Virginia financial community had previously known.

Sovran is the alternate and chiefly poetic spelling of the world *sovereign*. Its meaning focuses on several descriptive words and phrases: an acknowledged leader; unlimited in extent; enjoying autonomy and independence; superlative in quality, unsurpassed; strong, supreme, paramount; effective.

In late March 1984, less than three months following its formation, Sovran Bank, N.A. had more than double the name awareness of any other established financial institution in the state of Virginia. Research also showed that by the end of the first quarter of 1984, 96 percent of the consumers in Sovran's market area recognized the new organization's name.

Sovran owns the market in terms of unaided awareness of its name, as well as advertising awareness. In addition, the overall public relations program supporting the Grand Opening generated sufficient publicity to reach 82 percent of all households in Virginia during January 1984.

In the case of Sovran, the bank name must be followed by the term *N.A.*, a legal requirement that means "national association." Sovran Bank, N.A. is the principal subsidiary of the larger Sovran Financial Corporation. Additionally, the original Virginia National Mortgage Corporation merged into First & Merchants Mortgage Corporation, which changed its name to Sovran Mortgage Corporation. All consolidated financial statements had to conform to generally accepted accounting principles and to practices of the banking industry. These reclassifications, in addition, had to conform to the reporting practices of predecessor institutions and changes to adopt the Securities and Exchange Commission's revised bank holding company disclosure requirements.

Sovran's Logo

Besides the attention given choice of a name, Sovran devoted considerable energy to finding a suitable logo. The bank name, short and easy to read, lends itself to the logo and, in fact, constitutes a major part of it. The name, Sovran, appears in crisp, serif-style lettering. Its regal "V" drops below the line to touch lightly the apex of the "A" in the word "Bank" positioned below. A three-stripe accent is placed above the name and clarifies the entire image.

This striking red, white, and blue identifier appears sharp and clear when seen in black and white or in color—an added advantage when it appears in newsprint or in full-color promotional advertising. In all, its appeal rests on its crispness and its conveyance of leadership, strength, refinement, and tasteful simplicity.

A Slogan Showing Direction: "A Change for the Times"

In addition to the visual impact of sharpness that Sovran's logo provokes, it also conveys a feeling of moving forward. To further the idea of a bank with a future, the bank selected a slogan which not only promotes the idea of leadership, but makes customers feel there was a need for change. Rather than avoiding mention of the change in order to appease public resistance, Sovran turns the idea of change into an advantage. The slogan "A Change for the Times" makes customers feel that the merger benefits them, that the change was overdue, and that they should welcome it as an opportunity to become a part of a major financial institution.

Words like "new," "innovative," "leadership," and "change for the better" are mentioned in advertising literature. Yet the copy promoting change appears with mainstream America, Norman Rockwell–type pictures, which conjure up memories of American strength and tradition.

The coupling of the new without relinquishing the past strength of America's financial institutions teases customers to Sovran's threshold and soon ushers them inside. Clearly, Sovran portrays a change which Americans are supposed to like. One of Sovran's main objectives in handling customer relations during the merger was to make customers feel that the new bank would help them more than the old banks did. Sovran will manage the cutomer's money by providing financial leadership. The theme "A Change for the Times" and the sophisticated Sovran identifier demonstrate that the bank is prepared to change because the customer needs and wants the change.

Preparing the Customer

Sovran went to great lengths to prepare customers for changes which the merger caused, and quickly realized that the most effective way was to maintain direct contact with them. A special toll-free hot line was established for customer questions. Approximately thirty employees from the two merging banks were trained to man telephones and to provide customers with accurate information. The hot-line number was included in newspaper advertisements for customer accessibility. Because frequent customer contact was expected during the first three months after the merger, the hot line operated during normal banking hours and on Saturdays at the beginning of the program with the understanding that it would eventually be phased out.

Sample merger-related questions and answers were provided the hot-line staff during training. Questions included every relevant topic from "Will my checking account number change?" to "Where are branch offices of the new bank located?"

The first weeks of the merger (in January 1984) prompted over 3,000 telephone inquiries per week. Calls reached a peak of 902 inquiries on January 20, after which time they began to drop off. By early February calls were coming in at approximately half the frequency, and by mid-February they had halved again. In all, during the first nine weeks the hot line operated, the staff responded to 23,480 calls.

The direct customer contact provided by the hot line proved a major success. By February 24, William A. Branigan, vice president of Sovran Bank, was able to report "for the past week we had less than 10 calls concerning the merger." By anticipating and responding to customers' fears and concerns, Sovran was able to virtually erase worries about the merger in less than two months.

Preparing Employees

Another effective way in which Sovran avoided customer confusion was by preparing employees to handle merger questions. Soon after the merger became effective on December 30, 1983, Sovran Bank published its first issue of a monthly, eight-page employee newsletter, *Sovran Times*. The January issue carried articles which informed employees how to better relate to customer concerns and to better handle their questions. Articles such as "Customers to Benefit from New Products & Services" appeared. And "The Old and the New," comparing charges on checking, money market, and savings accounts in table form so that the old banks' and the new bank's charges could be viewed easily, helped employees comprehend changes and relate them to customers.

But aside from keeping employees informed about new policies so they can better serve the public, the newsletter also informs employees how they can pursue career goals through training programs and provides a training program calendar for employees interested in advancement. As a human interest feature, *Sovran Times* spotlights employees who recently married or experienced noteworthy accomplishments in a regular column called "You Oughta Be in Sovran Times," and it includes feature and how-to articles which relate directly to bank employees.

Advertising and the Public at Large

A change on the scale of the Sovran merger can be successful only with an advertising campaign that targets broad public acceptance. The advertising campaign launched by Sovran was aimed at all Virginia households and the business community at large.

In order to ensure favorable publicity, Sovran utilized both print and broadcast media. Print media became the major vehicle by which the bank penetrated Virginia households. Near the end of the first quarter of business following the merger, Sovran was able to report that the merger had prompted 194 articles in eighty-one newspapers circulated in Virginia. The broad news coverage, it is estimated, reached 83.70 percent of Virginia households.

Twelve articles about the merger circulated in six national publications including the *Wall Street Journal*. The extensive news coverage about the merger helped Sovran further its recognition in the business world.

Broadcast media coverage of the merger began in December and continued into February. Television was to become the primary medium for introducing the bank. Concentration of the introductory campaign ran for seven weeks beginning December 31, 1983. During the first two weeks of this introductory period, sixty-second commercials appeared on all major television networks. From the third week until February 5, thirty-second and ten-second spots were added. Sovran ended the introductory phase February 19 with thirty-second spots showing the bank as a major Winter Olympics sponsor.

Billboards and fourteen-feet by forty-eight-feet rotary boards lined highways to announce Sovran's arrival, and approximately 300 poster boards were displayed statewide in supermarkets and on outside panels of buses as well as in metro stations in Northern Virginia. Also, branch offices located in more than 100 Virginia communities were provided with handout literature and displays.

Perhaps the climax to the advertising campaign was the grand opening ceremonies on January 3, 1984. Opening day became the occasion for releasing 31,000 colorful helium-filled balloons with Sovran's logo boldly displayed on their sides. Dedication ceremonies were held and the striking red, white, and blue Sovran signs were unveiled. By the time the

February issue of *Sovran Times* appeared, it reported that the more than 9,000 employees had successfully pulled off the "miracle of our merger."

And perhaps more importantly, *Sovran Times* was able to report in that same issue that, according to Jim Kirkpatrick, director of investor relations at Sovran, initial indications from the investment community, security brokers, and security analysts were "very good, even better than had been expected." Even more, increased interest in Sovran Financial Corporation stock was becoming apparent. Sovran had successfully weathered the change and emerged as "the largest bank holding company in Virginia and one of the largest in the Southeast." As of June 30, 1984, Sovran Bank ranked thirtieth in deposits among the nation's 300 largest commercial banks.

The Miracle of the Merger

When institutions undertake a major overhaul, such as that of the merger which became Sovran Bank, their primary objective is to effect the change while remaining financially sound. Although Sovran is relatively new, it appears to have achieved this by turning the change to its advantage. Sovran used the occasion to establish a new image, to advertise its merger as beneficial to customers, and to make known to the financial world that Sovran had become a major banking institution. At the heart of Sovran's endeavors to achieve change was the high goal of coming out ahead rather than simply preserving and protecting the premerger reputation of the banks involved. Rather than project the idea that customers wouldn't even notice the change, Sovran projected the idea that customers would notice and would, in fact, be better off because of the change.

The financial bottom line, of course, will be written in years to come, but certainly Sovran's attention to its new image has given the bank the sure footing needed to establish itself as a major financial institution.

ARCHITECTURE AND LANDSCAPE DESIGN

Symbolic of the corporate image is the corporate headquarters and surrounding landscape. As mentioned earlier in this chapter, the producers of the soap *Dynasty* recognize the importance of corporate "good looks." Likewise, many business executives believe that in order to project an image of success, the corporate headquarters itself must appear successful. Communicated to all visitors, interior and exterior design create first impressions of the company's success. A new, distinctive thirty-six–story American Telephone & Telegraph building on Madison Avenue in New York City designed by Phillip Johnson reflects the style of earlier Manhattan buildings, yet in an updated style. The interior public space and elevated, expansive grand foyer convey the image of a corporation of longevity and substance, while simultaneously expressing newness and responsiveness to change.

In an effort to project a corporate image consistent with business lifestyles in the Southwest, and to express that image in materials reflecting the company's products, Southwest Forest Industries in Phoenix, Arizona, undertook a major project. Southwest insisted that the interior and exterioir design of its new 85,000 square-foot, aluminum-sheathed headquarters blend with and reflect the best of the surrounding environment. The new building, interiors, graphics, and landscaping have won awards, providing Southwest favorable visibility in the business community. The building's interiors benefit the company by encouraging maximum communication among employees, while maintaining personal privacy.

Corporate image has been a long-standing concern for the Italian office machine manufacturer Olivetti. According to writer Christiane Opperman, "Form and design have been the keynote of Olivetti since its founding in the early 1900's. The founder's son put an architect into the company's number two spot, and it was this architect, Marcello Nizzoli, who built Olivetti's corporate image and established its logo."

Opperman, writing in the German magazine *Manager*, recapped Olivetti management's concern for the corporate image.

A corporate identity crisis developed for a number of reasons when Nizzoli left, and another architect was appointed. A modern logo and well-defined corporate image were needed to extend over new product lines and express the personality, philosophy and product lines characteristic of the company. A new logo with contemporary lettering was developed for use throughout all subsidiaries—on letterhead, vehicles and packaging.[4]

Olivetti places such strong emphasis on corporate image that two architects are retained as design consultants. One specializes in the design of office furniture and computer equipment, and the other in electronic calculators and typewriters. As an additional responsibility, the design consultants negotiate with production, sales, and marketing department personnel to develop products which meet with the approval of public scrutiny. The total effort is coordinated to develop awareness of design preferences of mass markets.

WHEN A CHANGE IS DUE: SOME CONSIDERATIONS

AT&T, Southwest Forest Industries, and Olivetti are but a few corporations willing to expend extreme effort to modify or assert an image representative of their business endeavors and interests. When corporate executives question how well company exterior images effectively communicate what they want to project, many considerations and much planning must precede what can be a costly and time-consuming task.

Before undertaking a name, logo, or other corporate image change, one crucial consideration is whether the new image is necessary or whether a remedy rests elsewhere. Repositioning in the marketplace, for example, might give an organization necessary revitalization. A clothing manufacturer who has sold quality suits and hand-tailored shirts for a quarter of a century may suddenly need to rethink his marketing strategy in response to public trends, desires, and needs. Rather than a costly name and identity change, it may be wiser to sell glamour and confidence. Of course, such drastic repositioning often requires a modification of how the company represents itself in order to portray its new product line, but in some cases a total image change and the costs that accompany it can be avoided. The point is to consider various strategies and to survey market demands before taking the costly steps to project a new image.

However, sometimes developing a new image becomes the best approach in business improvement strategies. After all, like most things, identities grow old and stodgy. Modern business trends, style changes, altered business environments, all cause images to appear worn out or old-fashioned. In such cases, it is time to consider a major image change.

Contracting a marketing research firm to evaluate a product or service identity may be less costly and produce more professional results in the long run. Marilyn Ryan, vice president and director of strategy planning at Landor Associates in San Francisco, described how her firm's research provided guidance for Emery Air Freight Corporation. Faced with a loss in market position to Federal Express, the course of action for Emery involved, among other steps, renaming the company Emery Worldwide to emphasize the international aspect of the business. Just as important, ridding the company name of the word "freight" avoided the connotation of "slow-moving." Professional recommendations such as the Emery name change go far toward giving a corporation a boost and many corporate executives lack the time, expertise, and creativity necessary to resolve an image problem. Moreover, personal involvement in the company may blind executives to objective viewpoints.[5]

Hints from Those Who Have Undergone Corporate Facelifts

Nevertheless, occasions exist when corporate managers prefer a do-it-yourself approach to changing an image. Depending on staff time and budget size, market research and identity consultants may or may not be needed to spot identity problems. In a do-it-yourself, seven-step guide to investigate the possibility of a company's image problems, Elinor Selame, president of Selame Design and author of *Developing a Corporate*

Identity, offers these suggestions. After collecting all visuals such as stationery, forms, photographs of signs and vehicles, advertisements and promotional materials, house organs, and packaging, make these seven assessments:

1. Determine if the material you collected reflects the size and diversity of your organization.
2. Determine if the materials vary from unit to unit in their design connotations, hence presenting a disorganized image.
3. Determine if, collectively, your materials fail to project an image of a dynamic, organized company moving ahead with all bases covered.
4. Determine if your visuals look old, outdated, and inflexible.
5. Determine if you are projecting the full geographic scope of your business or if your visuals project a local and regional look when they should be showing a national organization.
6. Determine if your materials adhere to one graphic design system and look dynamic and synergistic rather than sterile and stagnant.
7. Determine if your semiautonomous subsidiaries retain separate identities or, as often preferred, are tied to the parent company's logo, name, and themes.[6]

Going It Alone

Before you reach a final decision to overhaul an outward visual image, you need to answer a number of cause-and-effect questions. What is, or will be, the public perception? How does the overhaul affect corporate divisions' sales, advertising, marketing, and public relations? What are the geographic limitations—local, regional, national, international, and multinational? And what is distinctive about the product or service you offer?

Modifying an existing image or developing a new one is a costly, time-consuming endeavor. Careful consideration and planning should precede such an undertaking. Norm Sklarewitz, business observer, suggests that before embarking on a corporate identity upheaval, you follow these sensible steps:

1. Get bids from several design firms.
2. Consider keeping the traditional elements of what you already have.
3. Know your objectives.
4. Set your budget limitations.
5. Choose a public relations firm that will talk with you and analyze your marketplace.
6. Make sure key executives understand and support the facelift.
7. And get names of reputable firms from professional design associations.[7]

A case in point that substantiates the need for these various steps is that of the Louisiana Pacific Corporation's spinoff company in Portland, Oregon. As the largest lumber producer of Louisiana Pacific, the Portland affiliate needed to establish a corporate identity.

Gerard Griffin, director of communications for the newly formed corporation, wanted a corporate signature (logo) visually strong enough to set Louisiana Pacific immediately apart from its twin and all other timber-based outfits. The logo had to be applicable to Louisiana Pacific's wood and paper products, and it had to work for future products, which might or might not be forest-based. Griffin first offered nominal fees to a dozen art studios and free-lancers to develop a logo.

According to San Francisco area public relations consultant Robert D. French, the new design "did the job of portraying the company's personality as management and employees saw it—aggressive and innovative with essential strength and harmony."

After gaining acceptance of the logo from company personnel, Griffin, with the help of a design studio, wrote a corporate graphics manual specifying ink, paper and paper size, position and color relationships of signature elements, divisional names, and product trademarks. The implementation was expected to occur over a long time period, and the phase-in process extended over a period of twelve to thirty-six months.

Griffin acknowledged, "A change in the hall mark is not a simple proposition. But when the possibility arises, the public relations department should be ready to take the leadership of a management team and get the job done."

What was Griffin's reason for undertaking the project in the first place? "Most members of a company's publics do not see the elegant 'From the Office of the President' letterhead or the embossed purchase order. Most see, in addition to advertising and packaging materials, which are expected to be professionally produced, the vehicles, buildings, and signs. And too often this is where the graphics standards are ignored."[8]

WHAT'S IN A NAME?

A company's name has the power to create and disseminate a picture of the company however and wherever necessary. The name carries the glory of success or the brunt of financial demise. Selecting a company name, or changing an existing one, should not result from whim, as the name change is expensive and takes a long time to saturate the public mind.

Company names may be repeated globally and become a staple of international vocabulary. The names Xerox, IBM, McDonald's and Mobil Oil are as well known as the name of a relative. To those inside and outside the corporation, the company name is the first source of identification and the primary carrier of the corporate image. Corporate identity is a basic vital element of a company's total communication effort.

In considering a name change, company executives should first decide if the company's current name advances or hinders communication objectives. Often, as a company expands or merges, the previous name no longer conveys an accurate description of goods and services, location and history, or function. An outdated name may actually thwart company communication objectives. This is especially true under the following circumstances:

1. If the old name no longer accurately describes the company's activities.
2. If the old name creates confusion with other firms.
3. If the name is undistinctive or unwieldy.
4. If the name is geographically limiting.
5. If outside factors adversely affect the old name.[9]

Ideally, a name enhances public recognition and market position. A large corporation with diverse products may wish to consolidate all products under one tag. Datsun cars, a division of the larger Nissan Corporation of Japan, decided to bear only the Nissan name, dropping the Datsun tag. By doing so, Nissan intends to meet its ambitious goal of 8.5 percent of the world car market by 1990. Nissan also hopes the realignment will give the corporation higher visibility in money markets, making it easier to raise funds to finance its growing overseas manufacturing. Car industry sources in North America estimate that switching the name and rebuilding the image in the public mind will cost some $150 million in new dealer designs and promotional material in the United States alone.[10]

Despite the astronomical amounts that must be budgeted for a name-change campaign, name changes are taking place at a rapid clip. More corporations changed their names in 1983 than in any of the fourteen years that Anspach Grossman Portugal has been tracking such activities. The design firm noted 1,055 name changes in 1983, an increase of 246 changes, or 30.4 percent. Of these, 52.3 percent resulted from mergers or acquisitions, and 47.6 percent of the changes were made by financial institutions, the largest group for the last nine years.[11]

Hal Goodman, business analyst, reminds us:

A name change can be a long, involved, costly procedure. Unfortunately, no cut-and-dried rules exist for undertaking a corporate name change. A major factor in a successful transition may lie in the old name itself . . . a new corporate name can bring both advantages and problems. The name should be easy to pronounce and understand over the telephone and look good on a letterhead. What the name inherently imparts as a communication device is essential; it should be distinctive, memorable, and contain a useful element that enhances communication. A good name is easy to spell, easy to pronounce, has no unfortunate connection either in the United States or overseas and clears legally, state by state.[12]

Goodman emphasizes two basic rules for a company to follow when choosing a company name. One, make the name memorable. Two, choose a name that reflects what the company does.

A company name can communicate to the public its dynamism, specialization, or diversification. Goodman advises, "Although computers can be helpful when selecting a new name, they sometimes generate a long list of possibilities. In 1983, when Hart Schaffner & Marx changed its name to Hartmarx, the firm used research and meetings with executives to determine a list of likely new names."

Goodman adds, "It can also be helpful to involve employees in the naming process." Involving employees in forming or modifying corporate identity not only taps many minds with various creativity levels, it makes the rank and file feel important, thus increasing morale.

Legal Considerations

Names and trademarks must be registered with the government. Registration procedures vary from state to state, and a corporate attorney or state attorney general's office can provide assistance with legal requirements.

The first advice in changing a corporate name is to seek legal counsel from the corporate legal staff. Special laws applicable to name changes govern within states, counties, or cities. A name change might require a special registration within a particular jurisdiction so no infringement on other names or identifiers occurs. The legal wrangle over the NBC symbol is an example of the difficulties encountered when conflicts occur.

If a name has been previously registered, in most cases the same name cannot be repeated. County or city courts maintain name registration sections or packets of instructions for registering a name. In most cases, a small fee must be paid.

Of course, incorporating for the first time is a special case requiring legal assistance. Kits for incorporation can be purchased at bookstores or in large business supply stores, but legal counsel is advisable in addition to these self-help materials.

CORPORATE IMAGES SHAPE PUBLIC ATTITUDES

Considerations mentioned in this chapter concerning outward symbols and outward appearance go far toward gaining public acceptance and respect. Vanity is not the reason corporations spend tremendous amounts of time and money creating an outward image to attract public attention. Corporate executives learned long ago that appearance shapes attitudes. When corporate executives are willing to cultivate public attitudes, the net gains are reflected in positive customer response, investment in the corporation, and community support—in short, growth and prosperity.

NOTES

1. Dennis J. Moran, "Corporate ID Is Your Major Resource," *Communicator's Journal* 1 (May/June 1983): 34–38.

2. Pat Allen, "Changing Institutions Seek New Identities," *Savings Institutions* 104 (July 1983): 52–56.

3. Written interview materials supplied by Mary D. Sellars, public relations officer, Sovran Bank, N.A. A special word of gratitude to her and Sovran Bank officials for sharing their thoughts included in this work.

4. Christiane Opperman, "Olivetti—The Secret of the Red Cassettes," *Manager Magazine* (Germany) (December 1982).

5. "Companies with Sagging Images are Bailed Out with New Corporate, Brand, or Product Identities," *Marketing News* 17 (October 14, 1983): 18–19.

6. Elinor Selame, "Keeper of the Mark," *Public Relations Journal* 37 (November 1981): 44–46.

7. Norm Sklarewitz, "The Corporate Image Calls for a Facelift," *Inc.* 4 (December 1982): 11–12.

8. Robert D. French, "Louisiana-Pacific's Do-It-Yourself Corporate Identity Overhaul," *Public Relations Journal* 37 (November 1981): 48–50.

9. Hal Goodman, "Name-Dropping," *Across the Board* 2 (May 1983): 35–39.

10. "Nissan's Zillion Dollar Decision to Kill the Datsun," *International Management* 37 (United Kingdom) (December 1982): 55.

11. "Name Changes Grew For Companies in 1983," *New York Times*, April 17, 1984.

12. Goodman, p. 36.

6

Management's Role: Beyond the Dollar Sign

Man is nothing till he is united to an image.

—William Butler Yeats

When Yeats wrote the above line, he was referring to a model or vision of what a man could become. The same can be said of corporations. But companies do not create images. People do. And chief executive officers are among the most likely candidates involved in the image-building process. From the chief executive officer to staff and line management, all are seen as carriers of the corporate image torch.

THE CHIEF EXECUTIVE OFFICER: CORPORATE IMAGE LINK

In a television special titled "Lee Iacocca—An American Profile," Iacocca was portrayed as the chief executive officer of Chrysler Corporation and as a private, family man. As a family man, Iacocca appeared sensitive, soft, kind, and dedicated to personal values.

Iacocca's virtues as a private man stand in almost direct contrast to his public image as the hard-as-nails, front-seat leader of an American auto manufacturer. Iacocca, whose language was so frequently peppered with four-letter words that, prior to televising the special, producers warned viewers they might find the language offensive, presented a dual image. Which image should the public believe?

At the core of both images is a chief executive officer who has led the Detroit automaker from the point of bankruptcy to a recovery in which Chrysler is paying a handsome dividend for the first time since 1979. Fired from Ford Motors, hired to lead Chrysler from its darkest hours, Iacocca successfully bid the federal government to bail out the auto company with nearly a billion dollars in loans—loans not only repaid, but repaid well in advance of the due date.

The Chrysler recovery story is intrinsically tied to Iacocca. Beneath the public guise, Iacocca analyzed the public's car-buying habits, offering the Chrysler market smaller, gas-efficient models. Against all the odds of turning Chrysler around, he persevered and won.

One strategy Iacocca initiated to implement a return to black ink was to recast Chrysler's image as responsive to the needs of American drivers. Iacocca's early ad campaign encouraging buyers to return to Chrysler sticks in the mind of the American people to this day. Iacocca's television and newspaper ads appealed to the potential buyer's sense of product reliability, safety, and patriotism. Although critics questioned the relationship between helping the American economy and making car-buying decisions, the appeal worked. The patriotic ingredient provided an added incentive to buyers. Automobile analysts suggest that without Iacocca's ads, the company's effort would have gone unnoticed. There were dark times during the image-rebuilding process when the business press roasted Iacocca and labor unions grew hostile. Yet Iacocca's daily mail was stuffed with thousands of letters supporting his stance. The campaign was a success for Chrysler and for Iacocca.

The Chief Executive Officer's Role in Corporate Image

Iacocca embodies the best of the new American chief executive officer and stands as a model for others. Despite public and media criticism, business leaders view him as a role model.

As in Iacocca's case, it is generally understood that chief executives are the central focus of public opinion of the corporation. Moreover, management from the chief executive officer down admits that public visibility can have a dramatically positive impact on how the public perceives a corporation. Corporate identity has come to rest on the shoulders of the chief executive officer and other top-rung managers. Just as the public associates Iacocca with Chrysler, it associates the former astronaut Frank Borman with Eastern Airlines; hotelier Bill Marriott with Marriott Corporation; and chicken king Frank Purdue with Purdue Corporation. The chief executive officer is the voice of the corporation, a voice that reflects the image of the entire organization.

In the role of corporate spokesperson, the chief executive officer assumes the burden of defining, molding, and communicating the corporate view. Part of the task is to assure that corporate policies are expressed in a way that reflects the corporation as a credible, open entity responsive to public expectations.

Despite the power and importance of the nation's corporate chief executives, a yawning disparity often exists between what the chief executive officer is in the public stereotype and what he is in reality. The widely held public view of chief executive officers is that they have one interest in mind—the profit motive. Public opinion, reinforced by television, believes that the chief executive gains power through profits, and power becomes his all-consuming ambition.

ARE PUBLIC AND MEDIA ACCUSATIONS JUSTIFIED?

An annual Louis Harris poll measuring public confidence in corporate executives showed that only 18 percent of those surveyed in 1984 placed "great confidence" in American executives—down from 29 percent in 1973 and 55 percent in the mid-1960s. Another poll by the Opinion Research Corporation found that only 29 percent of Americans in 1983 rated corporate executives "excellent or good" in ethical practices. That was down from 33 percent in 1981 and 36 percent in 1975.[1]

America's corporate executives are suffering from a reputation of being too greedy and concerned only for the rewards of business. The creation of new means to gain monetary reward is at the heart of the public hue and cry. Mergers and acquisitions are perceived as further encroachments of big business over the little guy. Two outgrowths of the recent takeover phenomenon also cause a ripple—"golden parachutes" and "greenmail." The golden parachute is a huge payment made to an executive after his departure from a company. Best known of the golden parachute rewards is the $4 million paid to Bendix chairman William Agee during the Bendix-Martin Marietta takeover battle.

The most-cited recent case of greenmail—rewarding a raider to leave a company alone by buying his stock at a premium price—occurred during the spring and summer of 1984. Walt Disney Productions fought to escape a takeover by Saul Steinberg's Reliance Group Holdings. Disney's management succumbed to Steinberg and paid the financier $325.5 million for his 11 percent stock in the company.[2]

Are such examples of business-leader excesses the rule? A general worry is a backlash toward business in general. "These mergers are destructive to the American business fabric," argues Bernard Rapaport, chairman of the American Income Life Insurance Company in Waco, Texas.[3]

The public seriously doubts that executives are even aware the common man exists. Worse, the public believes the business executive would sacrifice public interest and even public health in order to enlarge company coffers. In short, chief executive officers have failed to sell themselves to the public.

David Finn, chairman and cofounder of Ruder & Finn, Inc., one of the largest public relations firms in the world, writes in "Public Invisibility of Corporate Leaders" that chief executive officers "don't seem to know how to fire the public's imagination with enthusiasm and excitement about life's potentialities. They rarely inspire public confidence in their judgments about how to cope with great social problems. They don't propose goals for mankind to which all can aspire." Finn qualifies his assertions by adding:

This is not to belittle the value of the many social and cultural contributions which corporations have made in recent years. It is rather a commentary on the lack of credit business executives have received for these contributions and the responsibility of management itself for this failure. Instead of winning public respect for their many public services, business people have been condemned for the supposed venality of their motives, their lack of honesty, integrity, and character. . . . The good deeds [of corporations] are considered by many as little more than strategies to deflect attention from a company's antipublic policies—"charity to hide a multitude of sins," to quote Thoreau.[4]

To air these persistent misperceptions, Warburg, Paribas Becker, the international bankers and brokers, commissioned the Roper Public Opinion Research Center, Inc., to find out what chief executive officers think—as individuals, not as corporate spokesmen—about today's public perceptions and their own personal concerns and satisfactions.

Dun's Business Month published a sampling of their responses in the August 1982 issue. The anonymous quotes drawn from the Roper findings dispel the chief executive officer's image as unconcerned about society.

Comments on the Economy

"The ideal is to balance expenditures and revenues and at the same time treat people fairly—not disadvantage certain sectors. But it can't be done. As in war, you know there are going to be casualties, but you have to win."

"The American free-enterprise system is a model for the world, the engine that makes the world go. The engine is not broken; it just needs a few repairs."

Comments on Problems of Society

"Some believe that the work ethic is disappearing, that people don't give a damn. But I see a real dedication in many of our younger employees. There are many outstanding young kids, and I mean not just college graduates, but all young people."

"I wonder if our golden era isn't behind us. Expectations have been so unrealistic."

"The most fundamental problem that we face is an expanding population that has escalating material aspirations in a society that has finite resources."

Comments on Success and Its Costs

"It's all been fun, realizing not only your own potential, but helping others realize theirs. Motivating people. That's what I really enjoy. And that's what's important. I can't possibly do it all myself."

Comments on the Media

"One thing I do is spend a lot of time with the press. I think it's important to get the truth across—or what I perceive as the truth. Some of my best time is spent with young reporters."[5]

Given this backdrop, it's safe to assume that not all chief executive officers take a complacent or defensive posture. Some are deeply concerned. As business leaders, they are making inroads into the arduous process of regaining credibility and public trust. Naturally, business leaders, like other groups, tend to react defensively when blamed for the widespread loss of confidence society places in its institutions. Regaining credibility and public trust is going to take a sense of maturity and skill, but with the chief executive officers' changing responsiveness to public concerns, the load should prove lighter.

The public outcry for renewed business credibility is forcing the chief executive officer to consider a new agenda for the 1980s and beyond. W. H. Krome George, chairman and chief executive officer of Aluminum Company of America, puts it this way:

It is in large measure not a replacement of the agenda of previous decades, but a new list of things to which the [chief executive officer] must direct himself, while he also addresses those demands that have always been fundamental to his job. While this agenda is most visible in the performance of the chief executives of the largest corporations, it is increasingly a matter for a chief executive of any organization large enough to be visible to government and the public.

George continues:

The new agenda includes all the old qualities required of the [chief executive officer]: to know the economic, technological, and marketplace dimensions of the business and to be a manager, planner, and administrator. Indeed there have been changes in the nature of performance required in these roles; to a major degree, these new demands might also be considered as part of the new agenda. Furthermore, the chief executive must continue to "set the style" for his organization by providing ethical and moral leadership.[6]

MOLDING THE CORPORATE IMAGE—A SHARED RESPONSIBILITY

The function of leading the corporation, responding to public demand for credibility, and forging and communicating the corporate image should be shared with other members of management, including line management all the way to plant management level.

But too often, the major responsibility for answering to the public is left in the hands of the chief executive officer. Moreover, line and staff managers frequently avoid the issue. But corporate managers have begun to realize that leaders other than those at the top need to know about corporate public concerns and be able to answer to them. If the concern for social responsibility has become a high priority for top management, the same responsibility must sift downward. S. Prakish Sethi, director of the Center for Research in Business and Social Policy, School of Management and Administration, University of Texas, states, "Unfortunately, this concern for social responsibility has not yet penetrated the corporate hierarchy to line and middle management, especially managers who work in and are responsible for operating divisions in a company."

Sethi continues:

Line executives have difficulty relating their roles and operational responsibilities to the corporation's social involvement. Lacking a clearcut understanding of what the term implies, they tend to interpret it as a charitable gesture. Since line executives see themselves as "working in the trenches," they tend to assign a lower priority to directives on social issues. They view their jobs as primarily to insure that the economic activities of the company are carried out efficiently and profitably. Such attitudes are not limited to junior and middle-level managers, but also can be found among many senior managers.[7]

As Sethi emphasizes, junior and mid-level managers make decisions which have tremendous repercussions on the entire corporation. He gives examples of the insurance agent who refuses a homeowner's policy in a high-crime area or a loan officer who denies a mortgage loan in a high-risk neighborhood. From the viewpoint of the agent and the loan officer, these decisions are economically valid. But, as Sethi points out, they can result in lawsuits for discriminatory practices. The net result, as Sethi sees it, is that "line management clearly has a crucial role in a company's social impact."[8]

Participation from all management levels is paramount to implementing corporate objectives. To neglect inclusion of lower-level managers in corporate mandates results in lack of cohesion, which not only damages image, but possibly damages corporate integrity itself. When managers are given a clear view and unambiguous direction, the corporation is on its way toward successfully achieving its goals.

A first step is to realize that the corporation operates in a new environment—one that includes new demands from the public for social, as well as economic, accountability. The revised picture includes a downward shift in the values placed in business. The corporate culture now includes increased employee demands for job satisfaction and rewards.

If the corporation is seen at the center of numerous publics ready to lay blame at the corporate door for the slightest misdeed, the chief executive officer, buoyed by managers down the line, bears the brunt of defining and forging public perception of the corporation—a responsibility added to an already overly long list.

What Role Should a Manager Play?

First, managers should recognize that corporations are operating in a new environment—an environment that must include all social and cultural concerns. Though profit, the economic survival of the corporation, must remain a primary goal, the corporation is involved in a society that looks to it and its leaders as captains to steer society in the right direction. Even with the change in what Americans expect from institutions, business leaders are still expected to provide leadership.

Among themselves, managers must realize that their decisions shape the corporate culture, directly affecting the standing of the corporation and thus its image. In a world of ever-increasing competition, this places a demand on managers to be strong survivors, yet willing to accommodate inevitable change. The manager needs to know the image expected within the corporation, from senior leaders down to employees.

Employees might expect their managers to project an image of leader, but with a diminished sense of autocracy. Democratic and laissez-faire management styles are fast replacing the vintage autocrat as leader. Managers must now include the rank and file in decision-making policies. To shape a concerned image, a manager must demonstrate genuine concern while permitting employees the freedom to grow and compete professionally.

The changing social/cultural environment places demands on management that sift outward to the community and consumers. Business leaders are expected to be community leaders as well.

THE RESPONSE-PROGRAM STRATEGY

Corporate philosophy must consider social responsibility along with economic survival. Stop-gap measures must be replaced with long-range planning. Because managers are adding to the list of responsibilities, they must be given rewards and recognition.

The response may begin with a slight shift in attitude—to recognize the public cry for social responsibility. Because improving public perception of the corporation is one answer to the social responsibility problem, managers should give corporate image high priority as a corporate goal.

This may require extending the leadership scope. The new scope should consider the various publics and their expectations of business. Being an active and forceful spokesperson for the corporation is another requirement.

Understanding the components of corporate image and the way to communicate that image is one key, and specific steps are spelled out in the following chapters for improving these skills. Two goals are closely linked to the company's priority to succeed as an economic unit. One goal is to maximize the company's positive impact while minimizing the negative impact on employees, customers, and communities. The second is to participate in solving pressing societal problems.

Formally, a firm expresses its social role through the company media—the annual report, press releases, speeches, and other media geared to external publics. Informally, the firm makes an image statement each time it lays people off, closes a plant, contributes to a charity, or encourages volunteerism among employees. Examples of innovative internal communication devices are given in Chapter 8.

A sound beginning for an internal strategy includes:

1. Establish a positive work setting that encourages open communication. Face-to-face dialogue among and across employee levels is the best channel. Interpersonal communication should not be replaced by less personal media such as newsletters and audiovisuals.

2. Target communication to important employee subgroups. A three-minute, informal accolade at the departure of an employee can do as much to enhance corporate and personal goodwill as an expensive luncheon or dinner without the words of appreciation. Employees pick up on and remember the good deed.

3. Design messages to help employees better understand the corporate citizenship role. Media such as the newsletter or annual report should include articles extolling corporate efforts toward maintaining goodwill.

4. Help employees understand their jobs in terms of the total corporate mission. A new employee may be particularly frustrated and develop a negative attitude, if left to compete without the benefit of knowing why. Attracting and retaining quality employees hinges on setting an appropriate positive perspective about company philosophy and objectives.

5. Encourage employees to make suggestions. Well-run companies offer incentives and rewards for outstanding contributions. One company makes annual outstanding employee awards at a banquet honoring recipients and their families company-wide. Vacations, time and expenses, or a bonus can make the competition more worthwhile.

6. Senior management should remain visible and accessible to all employees. Some companies stress the ideas of family and team.

7. Encourage employee volunteer groups. Set aside work time for employees to get involved in a local civic or charitable drive.

8. Invite local political or government figures as speakers. This act advances healthy political activism while educating employees about the realities of political and governmental life.

9. Provide outside training and educational opportunities to show concern for career growth. Companies pay for all or a percentage of outside education expenses. Other companies contract with universities or consultants to provide in-house programs.

10. Analyze volatile situations to get at the root causes. Employee dissatisfaction may rest in reasons underlying the surface expressions of malcontent. Asking for anonymous written reasons is one way to uncover unhappy feelings.

If internal communication strategy receives priority, so must external. As a manager, you may sometimes feel like a go-between, balancing internal concerns with external. Paramount to both efforts is a willingness to do your best and to realize that even a minimal effort will make a large contribution toward bolstering the corporate image.

A sound beginning for an external communication strategy includes:

1. Look to the long-range view. Too often a strategy is lacking completely, is designed to handle only short-term emergencies, or is established only after the company has faced a crisis.

2. Include in the plan yardsticks for constant reevaluation. What works today may not work tomorrow. Be prepared for change.

3. When a tragedy or crisis strikes, communicate openly and honestly. Johnson & Johnson's handling of the Tylenol crisis (Chapter 3) is living proof of the wisdom of this advice.

4. Choose corporate spokespersons carefully. Remember, those in the public eye are a direct reflection of the corporate image. Spokespersons should be knowledgeable, confident, poised, and accurate. My first book, *The Winning Image*, deals in-depth with personal presentational style. If those chosen for public visibility lack necessary attributes to appear before the public, they should receive training in public image and speaking techniques.

5. Establish a central communications or media office. Coordinate all public announcements through this office. (Refer to the next chapter, ''Media Relations: Conveying a Consistent Public Image,'' for details.)

6. Some corporations publish annual social responsibility reports. These can prove a thorn unless every issue presented is thoroughly researched and presented without bias. The company must be willing to spell out its social performance standards and role.

7. Become involved in community groups and volunteer programs. Such activities spread goodwill.

8. Strive to gain political and governmental expertise. Become active in a local campaign or party affiliation of your choice.

9. Join professional associations to enhance credibility and make your name known. This promotes the company's reputation, too.

10. Strive to produce a quality product or service. The product or service is the link to the customer. Economic survival, as well as the reputation of your company, may well hinge upon this point alone.

The task of a company communicator includes every facet of the corporation that impacts upon the public. The challenge is to understand how the roles of internal and external communication strategy overlap and how they directly shape the corporate image.

This chapter presents the underpinning for your strategy. Successive chapters help you determine how you and your company can best act in enlightened self-interest. Conveying well-planned messages to your publics, inside and outside the company, safeguards corporate image.

NOTES

1. Ann Crittenden, "The Age of 'Me-First' Management," *New York Times*, August 19, 1984, p. 1F.

2. Ibid., p. 2F.

3. Ibid., p. 12.

4. David Finn, "Public Invisibility of Corporate Leaders," *Harvard Business Review* 58 (July 1982): 102–110.

5. "The CEO Speaks Out," *Dun's Business Month* (August 1982): 60–66.

6. W. H. Krome George, "The CEO's New Agenda," in *The Public Affairs Handbook* (New York: AMACOM, 1982), pp. 7–9.

7. S. Prakish Sethi, "Battling Antibusiness Bias: Is There a Chance for Overkill?" *Public Relations Journal* 37 (November 1981): 25–27.

8. Ibid., p. 26.

7

Media Relations: Conveying a Consistent Public Image

"*60 Minutes* calling. Our reporter would like to ask you a few questions. . . ."

A telephone call like that or mention of the name Mike Wallace might prompt a slightly audible sound of shaking knees in the corporate boardroom. Only a sliding profit margin is likely to elicit a similar response. Carlton Spitzer, APR, a Washington, D.C.–based public affairs counselor, puts it best. He notes:

An invitation to be interviewed by Mike Wallace on 60 Minutes—the popular CBS television news magazine—puts jelly in the bones of any chief executive officer. The name Mike Wallace is, for many, synonymous with exposé. By his own standard, and in the opinion of most of his peers, he is a top-flight investigative journalist. But to fearful business (and government) officials, he is a hatchet man.[1]

Media coverage of an organization has a significant positive or negative impact. Public perception of the organization and the confidence and support the public places in it are often determined by the treatment received in the press, especially on radio and television. S. Prakish Sethi, author of a book on corporate free speech, remarks:

In a democratic society, an institution's legitimacy is greatly influenced by the public perception and acceptance of that institution's societal role and activities. Surveys show that an overwhelming majority of people get their news from TV. Seventy-five percent of the viewing public watch the three networks' programs during prime time. Television is also the primary source of alleged distortions and inaccuracies in the coverage of business news and negative portrayals of those in business.[2]

Corporations in such industries as energy, chemicals, minerals, metals, and forestry products have been especially bitter about their treatment in network news programs.

HOW SHOULD CORPORATIONS RESPOND?

It is obvious that the media, television especially, are important in making and breaking corporate images. Corporations can improve their images by establishing a rapport with various media. To achieve this, corporate spokespersons and public relations officers should work toward the following goals.

Overcome the fear of media by facing media and sharing information. Promote sound relations with media representatives and give them consistent, honest answers to their queries. Establish a central media relations office which openly responds to the media. And reinforce the central office with a network of spokespersons from the chief executive officer to supervisors and down the line. Make sure this network gives honest, consistent responses to media inquiries. Notice that the word *consistent* is stressed time and again. Lack of consistency is a major complaint from media representatives.

When the needs of the mass media and journalists are understood, and when organizations prepare to deal with those needs, print and broadcast media become valuable resources for organizations to promote favorable public images. If the media are not understood and if organizations are ill-prepared to deal with the media, they can be dangerous. Good media relations are the result of good organization operations and management. The well-run organization, fulfilling its appropriate social goals, can only be aided by attention given it by the media.[3]

MEDIA PHOBIA—REAL OR IMAGINED?

The media, television news magazines in particular, appear to have painted a not so rosy image for business and business leaders. The tarnished image results in fear of media exposure. In many cases, business fear of the media seems unfounded. According to a study by Brouillard Communications, the much-publicized antagonism between business and broadcast news media may be more myth than reality. Survey findings show that "more corporations are turning to radio and television news interviews to articulate corporate policy . . . and corporate spokesmen are treated 'fairly' in almost all interviews."[4]

The Brouillard study queried top communications officers of the 1,300 largest corporations as ranked by *Fortune*. The questionnaire elicited a 30 percent response rate. Of the 395 respondents, 245 (62 percent) said that "one or more senior executives in their company had participated in a broadcast news interview during the past 18 months." Two in five respondents said their executives had been treated *fairly* during *every* interview, while the remaining three felt their executives had been treated *fairly* during *most* interviews.

John Higgins, vice president and public relations director of Brouillard, comments, "We believe this finding does not reflect a mellowing by news organizations or a slackening in vigilance. Instead, we think more and more top corporate executives have learned what their rights are in a news interview and are using this information to their advantage."

Of great significance is this finding:

Current company policy, said 72 percent of respondents, favors using broadcast interviews to communicate company policy; only 15 percent said company policy was opposed. Furthermore, more than 60 companies said this policy had changed to pro-interview during the past five years, while only seven companies said the policy had changed the other way.[5]

Contrary to popular thought about fear of the media, business and media now appear to be striving for mutual understanding and respect. A completely harmonious relationship may never be achieved, and may be an unrealistic corporate goal. Writing in *Democracy in America* more than one hundred years ago, Alexis de Tocqueville perhaps best states the rule that still applies. "To enjoy the inestimable blessing of a free press, it is necessary to endure and tolerate the evils that a free press will engender; to believe one can enjoy the first without suffering the second is to indulge in illusion."

Washington-based public affairs counselor Carlton Spitzer continues by observing:

Business fears the media and usually acts accordingly. It is time for both adversaries to clean up their houses and to develop a more productive relationship. . . . In the 80s, business and media executives seem to agree on at least two major points: the media must perform more responsibly, business must be more open and accessible.[6]

THE BUSINESS/MEDIA ALLIANCE

To allay fear of media, a first step is to realize that the media, including television, radio, magazines, and newspapers, are themselves businesses and that they face the same problems as any other business. The mass media of the United States are part of the corporate world. Most obviously, the mass media are profit-seekers that offer information as a commodity. Just as business competes in the marketplace of goods and services, so media compete in the marketplace of ideas and information.

Our economic well-being as individuals and as a society depends on a free flow of information. Rather than being the point of commonality between business and media, this point divides the two. The division is subtle, but has similar implications in terms of defining public perception and social responsibility. Basing their editorial conception of doing common good on the First Amendment right to free speech, media representatives claim they are watchdogs safeguarding the public interest. This role extends over government, business, and other major public, societal institutions. This role works fine as long as business and media perceive their social responsibility role in the same light. Division results when media and business perceive conflicting social responsibilities.

The complaint against the media is that their mutual goals of making a profit and providing the truth are often in conflict. They sell information. They gather and package information in such ways that audiences will be sufficiently interested to spend money or invest time to read, listen, or watch.

The same complaint is often registered against journalists, particularly news reporters. They perceive themselves as taking on a sacred public mission: to serve as the public's eyes and ears; to be watchdogs on public institutions doing the public's business; and to seek the truth, put it in perspective, and publish it so that people can conduct their affairs knowledgeably.

Journalists' devotion to these conflicting goals may cause their view of facts to be different from that of those who provide information. To the journalist, news is a highly perishable commodity. The source is more likely concerned with the lasting impression a news story makes. To the journalist, a story is a transient element in the ongoing flow of information. The news source is more likely to consider a story about the corporation as a separate, highly influential event affecting public image.

Casting the story or event in a negative light results in a negative public image; casting the story or event in a positive light results in a positive image. The journalist is usually not interested in the positive or negative flavor—just as long as facts are accurately presented.

Yet examples of antibusiness bias abound. The accusation from business is that media create their own definition of facts or omit facts that do not support their point of view. In some cases, the accusation appears justified. Television appears especially guilty. Robert Ristau and Kathleen Wilson, media specialists, write in an article in *Management World*:

The negative attitude of the public toward business in general is reinforced by television, which often portrays business in a negative fashion. A report from the Media Institute indicates that the redeeming social value of business is not apparent on TV. Businesspeople often are depicted as foolish, greedy, or criminal, and business is almost never shown as socially useful or economically productive. Businesspeople are rarely shown as making any contributions to the social or economic well-being of their communities. Although TV is not inherently antibusiness, the problem of the image of business it conveys is real.[7]

THE BUSINESS RESPONSE: A CONSISTENT MEDIA PROGRAM

Combating the negative image of business portrayed by the media has itself become a business. Countless books and expensive seminars advise corporate executives how to respond to a hostile interviewer. Knowing how to deal with hostile media might be a valuable skill every manager needs to know. However, the effort usually treats the wound after the blood has been let. The attempt is often remedial rather than preventive.

Keeping the corporate image intact requires more than bandages. Public scrutiny and the open eye of the watchdog press demand an answer for accountability. Loss of public confidence must be restored by a willingness of business to work with the media. Gone are the days when business executives could maintain a low profile. Corporate actions are a concern of the public and the press. Business executives should work hard at improving their performance in working with the media. It is business's responsibility to learn to deal with the news media and to live with some of their deficiencies.

Part of the answer lies in a corporate media program that answers to the public and to the media. The program design must openly, honestly, and consistently respond to public concerns. The word *consistent* cannot be overly stressed. Lack of consistency appears to be the major gripe from the media. For example, a reporter telephones the corporate headquarters in New York, then contacts the manufacturing plant in Omaha, and gets different sides of the same story. Faced with a problem of quality control, a defective product, water or air pollution, or other newsworthy item, managers must realize that bungling the potential media story affects everyone who knows the corporation, from employees on the inside to the community, consumers, and the general public on the outside. Given the best intent, a certain amount of misrepresentation will still take place. But consistent replies help allay distortion and inaccuracy.

A corporate media program design must include two basic steps to preserve a favorable corporate image.

Establish a corporate media or communications office. Assign all media relations responsibilities to the communications office. Duties include appointing a network of corporate spokespersons, keeping them up-to-date on corporate policy and events, and ensuring that information fed to the media flows to all personnel involved. The spokespersons should establish sound contacts with media; maintain current addresses and titles of media contacts; arrange news conferences and briefings; prepare, write, and disperse news releases and features; train or hire consultants to coach the spokesperson network in media relations; and in how to handle interviews and conflict situations.

The person appointed to run this office must know media practices and be familiar with successful public relations procedures. Former reporters, communication professors, or public relations personnel are likely candidates.

Another duty of the communications office is to inform management throughout the organization that all media contacts must be cleared through this central office. Press releases and news features originate here. This office arranges meetings with reporters and news conferences. Responsibility further includes maintaining a current media contact file. Annual media directories can be purchased and frequently used names entered into a computer or into a card file for easy access.

Bacon's Publicity Checker (Bacon Publishing Company, 14 E. Jackson Blvd., Chicago, IL 60604) has national listings. *Hudson's Washington News Media Contacts Directory* (2814 Pennsylvania Ave., NW, Washington, DC 20007) lists media personnel in the nation's capital. Similar directories are available for other cities and regional media centers.

Great care must be given to news clearance. For example, in Richmond, Virginia, a story breaks that has potential damage to the corporate image nationwide. The local paper demands a response. You explain that all media are handled through corporate headquarters in Los Angeles. The reporter persists, but you insist that he call Los Angeles. If the story is deemed important enough, the reporter will call Los Angeles.

A potentially damaging story creates a critical time when office politics and power battles must be put aside. Feeding the press conflicting or confused information not only causes you to lose credibility, but it harms corporate image.

Another duty of the central media office is to feed spokespersons in local offices. An office in Richmond, Houston, or Moline should have a spokesperson. Should a story break, local office personnel should maintain direct contact with the regional spokesperson, advising him of developments as they occur. This enables the regional spokesperson to respond honestly, knowingly, and responsibly.

Your network must be fed up-to-the-minute information. For routine news, news releases or memos suffice. These may need clearance through the corporate legal department. Morning or afternoon conference calls or electronic mail speed messages. Crises demand special updates. Frequent telephone exchanges become necessary and face-to-face meetings are preferable whenever possible.

Interviews and press conferences are two times when direct encounter with the media reflects your image. Look at these occasions as opportunities to create a positive image for your organization. A first step is to put information in positive tones, ridding comments of signs of a defensive attitude. Keep in mind that you have taken the time to establish sound relations and media contacts. If you have done this successfully, your chances of encountering a hostile press are lessened.

Establish contacts with the media. It is preferable to establish media contacts before an incident occurs. Don't wait for the media to contact you during a crisis. Feed the media consistent, honest answers to their queries.

Keep the media informed. Most reporters respect corporate spokespersons who become reliable and cooperative sources of information. If a reporter knows you can be relied on for honest answers, you will be called upon. Draw the line between becoming a substantial provider of information and an irritant. Reporters usually like to know you are available, but may not respond to a force-feed or constant attempt to get your news reported.

Face-to-face meetings reinforce the image by showing openness and willingness to communicate. Invite the local media into your organization for a tour or a special event. Be attentive, but avoid guiding the reporters. Let them form their own opinions. Provide a media kit, brochures or other supplemental information to accompany these personal meetings. Keep the media, especially local media, updated about corporate events. Provide a calendar of newsworthy events.

Be cautious about asking a reporter to lunch or dinner. The same holds true for offering travel tickets, gifts, or other freebies. The general rule is that if the item is part of the event coverage, it is acceptable. However, irrelevant gifts for other special occasions are questionable. Most media representatives set their own ethical standards. Overstepping their standards can lose a valuable contact and prove a detriment to positive relations that otherwise positively reinforce your corporate image.

An established, up-to-date corporate media or communications office and established media contacts need to be supported with knowledge of media basics—how to conduct press conferences and how to prepare to meet the press. There is no substitute for actual training, and a host of programs and consultants are available.

In selecting a training program, consider the investment. Most media consultants are expensive and many lack appropriate credentials. Colleges and universities, on the other hand, offer continuing education seminars at a fraction of the cost with training every bit as good as that provided by a former broadcaster turned consultant. Shop before selecting a consultant or program. Ask for credentials, background experience, and endorsements from previous clients.

The remainder of this chapter presents guidelines for conducting press conferences and responding to press inquiries. These guidelines provide an introduction to establishing a sound media image strategy.

Organization and Timing: Keys to a Successful Press Conference

Organization and timing are two keys to conducting a successful press conference. Provide background through media kits prior to a press conference. If broadcast media attend, select a well-lighted, spacious conference area that accommodates everyone comfortably. Television and video cameras may require special outlets or electrical hookups. It may become necessary to hire a technician to help with lighting, monitors, or microphones. Keep the conference area free from clutter. Arrange for a podium or speaker's platform that can also be used to display products. Slightly elevated platforms provide everyone a good view and aid camera people.

Provide a suitable backdrop. White walls cause shadows and wash out video shots. Flags, flowers, or a banner with the corporate logo create aesthetic visuals. If seating is provided, arrange chairs in a semicircle to ease eye contact and invite question-answer conversation. The semicircular arrangement also tends to create a slightly less adversarial atmosphere. When introducing a new product line, provide a sample product if feasible. If you are expanding, provide a building model or blueprint. Make sure reporters walk away with an 8 x 10 or 5 x 7 black-and-white glossy to include with a feature story. Provide a recording secretary who can mail a follow-up manuscript of the conference and supply additional pictures or models. A light lunch may be appropriate if the conference is scheduled in late morning or early afternoon.

Start and close on time. Assemble in an outer reception area and move into the conference room as a group. Providing coffee and light refreshments is appropriate for early morning conferences. Avoid entering and leaving the room after a conference is underway. Opening and closing doors wreak havoc for tape recorders and video cameras.

After the conference, provide an escort to the building exit. Assure reporters you will remain available during certain hours for a day or so after the conference to answer additional questions.

Preparation and Briefing: Keys to Successful Television Appearances

The following tips help prepare spokespersons for appearing before television cameras.

1. *Prepare.* Never "play it by ear." Whether you have three months or three hours lead-time, prepare.

2. *Think.* Sit down, take the phone off the hook, and think. Even the friendliest interviewer has an angle and at least one devil's-advocate question. Plant this idea firmly in your mind: "I'm going to say what I want to say, not what the interviewer wants me to say."

3. *Get a positive message across.* Although the gist of an interview may be negative, your responsibility is to turn the picture around. Employees may be losing jobs because of company cutbacks. On the other hand, you're still paying taxes, making a useful product, and making other contributions.

4. *Emphasize the positive.* It's easy to forget that your audience is not as familiar with your corporation as you are. Repeat the strong points about your organization.

5. *Coordinate.* An interviewer will seize upon conflicting points of view from the same organization. Coordinate policy statements and positions with the public affairs department. Coordinate with other executives or spokespersons representing your organization. Arrange a briefing or conference call to make sure views expressed to the media are in line.

6. *Protect yourself.* Ask your public relations staff to forward copies of memos, reports, newspaper clippings, and other information to you. Create a file that updates changing stances on issues. Refer initial reporter inquiries directly to the corporate media or communications office.

7. *Plan what you will say to the interviewer.* Think in terms of headlines. Write down your basic argument or stand on an issue. If you want to get several points across, condense them to a basic message. For example, "We are all aware of the potential pollution problem. But we are dedicated to providing jobs, producing quality products, and monitoring pollution levels."

8. *At best you can get three points across in an interview.* Make these three points the basis of everything you say. Whatever the questions, whatever message you want to convey, and whatever angle you decide on, get your basic points over to the viewer.

9. *Each of your three main points must stand on its own.* Three is an optimum number. Two, or even one main point, may well be all you have time to cover.

10. *Distill your message as much as possible.* Create one central theme. Use this theme throughout your appearance.

11. *Remember the limited time and immediacy of television and radio.* What it boils down to is that you will have an average of about two minutes to get your message across.

12. *Remember audience attention and receptivity.* Keep your message simple. Give examples and illustrations. You're competing for attention of an audience awareness level which is low. It's more effective to say the same thing several times than to say several things only once.

13. *Illustrate your point.* Use anecdotes, analogies, examples, and illustrations to get your message over. People love stories. They stick in the mind. Sup-

port the story with facts and statistics. For example, when describing the size of a new plant, you might say it's several thousand square feet. A substitute with immediate impact: "It's the size of a baseball field."

14. *Consider the reporter's angle.* Journalists know that audiences are bored with the whole picture. A slant adds interest.

Keys to Answering Questions

There are two ways to get an idea of the questions you might be asked if you are interviewed by the press.

First, you can ask the program producer. Or watch the program repeatedly to familiarize yourself with the types of questions generally asked. Some interviewers and producers will ask you to submit a set of questions. They center the interview around your list, but are unlikely to stay with it word for word.

Second, put yourself in the interviewers' shoes. Their job is to entertain and inform people. Pretend for a moment you know nothing about your topic, yet you have the responsibility of presenting it to the public. From this perspective, you can expect questions like these:

1. What do you or your organization hope to achieve?
2. How is help being provided?
3. How many employees or members of the community are affected?
4. What makes you think you're the right person for the job of addressing the issue? Your credentials are likely to be questioned.
5. What's your organization going to do, in practical terms?
6. Questions that deal with the what, why, where, when, and how of the issue.

You can make your point regardless of the question by following these suggestions:

1. Evade the question slightly. A favorite political ploy, the trick is incredibly simple. Answer the proposed question briefly, then go directly to your prepared answer.
2. Put the question into perspective or create a new perspective. Question: "How can you account for the large percentage, now over 50 percent, of unemployment among black males?" Answer: "Let's put the percentage in perspective. The summer months always bring higher unemployment rates, especially among employable high-school and college-age students. The growing numbers of illegal aliens also figure into that percentage."
3. Don't be afraid not to answer a question. Phrase your response: "I don't want to misrepresent myself or my company. I'll be happy to research your question and get an answer back to you."

4. Reporters have long memories so don't just drop a question or neglect to provide an answer. If you do, the first question you will get next time will be the forgotten one.

5. A simple, effective technique is a learned one that takes practice. Think of something you would say if you were given fifteen seconds of free television time. Think of the nastiest, most loaded question about your subject. Put the two ideas together.

6. Watch the pros. Practice comments like "I can't really answer that question without first explaining the background." "That's a good question and I'll return to it in a few seconds." "Let's just go back for a moment to reiterate your earlier question."

Good media relations should not be taken for granted. To gain full and positive impact from the media, you must cooperate with media representatives and adequately prepare for media events.

NOTES

1. Carlton E. Spitzer, "Fear of the Media," *Public Relations Journal* 37 (November 1981): 58–62.

2. S. Prakish Sethi, "Battling Antibusiness Bias: Is There a Chance of Overkill?" *Public Relations Journal* 37 (November 1981): 22–24.

3. Craig E. Aranoff and Otis W. Baskin, *Public Relations: The Profession and the Practice* (St. Paul, Minn.: West Publishing Co., 1983).

4. Carlton E. Spitzer, "Media: The CEO's Bogeyman," *Public Relations Journal* 37 (November 1981): 58–62.

5. Ibid., p. 62.

6. Ibid., pp. 58–59.

7. Robert A. Ristau and Kathleen Wilson, "Network Negatives: TV Gives Business Bad Ratings," *Management World* (June 1983).

8

Internal Corporate Image: Employee Concerns

Thinking ahead to the year 2000, how do you envision changes that will take place in your company and in your job? With the turn of the century and the coming millennium, futurists predict dramatic change in the workplace and the job market. The transformation in the workplace demands that the future successful manager will not only know how to spot change, but can continue to manage employees who expect greater personal satisfaction.

Employees who are intimately involved with the company are a valuable asset and should be treated as such. When employees take pride in their organization, they communicate their positive feelings to the public. Consequently, it is important to nurture goodwill among employees. Communicating openly is one of the most effective ways of promoting healthy employee relations. Neglect in this area usually spells future employee/management derision—an image which projects broadly. Employees are an organization's primary public and they should be both respected and treated with fairness. To expect a positive public image when employees complain throughout the immediate community and beyond is unrealistic. But employees whose concerns are taken into account and who are consulted about company policies and goals generally broadcast job satisfaction into the community at large.

CORPORATE CULTURES

Employee expectations of the near future underscore the need to understand corporate culture and its place in the corporate image picture. Companies operate under guidelines that are spelled out and adhered to by employees. Equally important are the rules that employees live up to that are not necessarily spelled out. These expected rules help shape the corporate culture and image. For example, a 9:00-5:00 workday may be written in the employee policy manual, but the expectation of a 9:00-7:00 workday may reflect actuality. Employees may work in a team demanding that they abide by the rules of the group. Yet, within that same group, individual members are expected to compete and develop a sense of independence and personal style.

To adapt to the cultural expectations, employees must pick up on these cues to gain acceptance. Reading the cues correctly may contribute to their success in the corporation. These cues are an inherent part of the corporate image.

The forces that shape corporate culture also shape the corporate image. Geographic location readily comes to mind. Business consultants who travel to the South, Midwest, or West talk about adapting to regional business expectations. Wearing a three-piece pinstripe and making a formal, stilted presentation are unlikely to wash well in Denver or Los Angeles. The cultural expectation is apparent.

The cultural expectation is secondary to recognizing that a corporation develops and operates its own culture. And this culture bears direct influence on the corporate image. To understand corporate image, managers should give some thought to the culture. Business writer Kristin von Kreisler-Bomben makes the point, "Like all societies, individual corporations have identifiable cultures subject to many influences. Certainly where you work helps determine how you work."[1]

Location and expected subtle behavioral cues are two components of corporate culture that shape corporate image. The employee who shifts cultures may not readily adapt to the new environment, and the failure to adapt quickly may prove a hindrance to that person's success. For instance, the competitive easterner may need time to acclimate to the laid-back western style.

Managers should consider the company's operating environment and its effect on employees. A negative effect can directly influence employee morale, job satisfaction, and productivity.

Futurists maintain that employees will continue to enter the work force with broad expectations and a new definition of work. These same futurists point to the acceptance of home workstations, called electronic caves by some. One view is that we will work directly from our homes, forfeiting the human interaction of the office. Working alone, workers of the next decade may substitute human interaction for a computer monitor or video screen.

In answer to the shift toward dehumanization in the workplace, corporations are responding with employee programs offering greater work incentives. Rewards offered are a means of motivating employees to accept automation and change. Workers need to feel involved in corporate

decision making and feel compensated for their work. In answer to the
loss of human interaction, many corporations now turn to the team con-
cept, to flextime, to stock incentives, and to benefits packages. Whatever the changes of the next decade and a half, corporations and their
managers appear more aware of the obligation to employees.

Employees, the bearers of internal corporate image, directly reflect the
corporation and carry the corporate message to the business community
and other vital publics. Roy Foltz, vice president and director of Tow-
ers, Perrin, Forster, and Crosby, states, "The most credible spokespersons for an organization are rank-and-file employees—not CEOs [chief
executive officers], VPs [vice presidents], and other top managers."

Foltz continues:

Rather than recognizing the comprehensive nature of employee communication,
public relations has traditionally viewed employees as one of many publics. In
some ways, employees are still viewed as a "public," but a very special one.
Public relations has recognized that employees are a medium through which other
publics gain information and establish attitudes toward organizations.[2]

Good relations with a community where an organization's facilities are
located or with the general public originate with good employee communications. A Gallup poll revealed that each employee influences an
average of fifty people in the community. Neighbors, family, friends, and
associates of employees are themselves potential customers, employees,
and decision makers on issues crucial to the organization.[3]

Just how effective are employees in advancing the social/corporate
cause? David Johnston, director of Public Policy Associates, points out,
"Evidence suggests that increasing numbers of managers are deliber-
ately engaging employees in dialogue, and that productivity and profits
tend to be high at firms that have open, participative management styles."

Johnston cites several examples of innovative vehicles to show management's concern for employee communication. Sperry Corporation in-
stituted "listening seminars" for employees, especially those who deal
with customers. The company has been publicizing the program in low-
key advocacy advertisements. Texas Instruments, once described by
Business Week as having Japanese-style management, uses attitude surveys unconventionally. Instead of handing employees a summary, department heads and branch managers receive raw results and discuss them
with workers. Then a committee of nonmanagement employees analyzes
them and makes detailed recommendations.

Bank of America, with nearly 80,000 employees and 1,100 branches,
uses an extensive employee feedback program. Potentially major problems are handled with attitude surveys, a confidential open line for rais-
ing questions about policies, and a corporate ombudsman. Other forums

include a Junior Advisory Council to discuss middle-management concerns, a Senior Officers Call Program in which a senior officer visits every unit periodically, and an extensive privacy policy.[4]

Uncovering Employee Concerns

The crucial prerequisite for effective employee relations and communication is the creation of a positive organizational climate based on feelings of trust, confidence, and openness. In effect, organizational climate consists of the subjective perceptions held by employees of such realities as policy, structure, leadership, standards, and rules. The primary responsibility for organizational climate belongs to line management, from the chief executive officers to supervisors. Staff must consistently stress and practice the need for two-way communication. Communication policies must be goal-oriented rather than event-oriented. They should focus on gaining employee understanding and identification with organizational objectives and problems.[5]

Scott Paper Company conducted a Community Needs Assessment to determine the kinds of information various groups of employees want; types of channels through which they usually receive information; strengths and weaknesses of those channels; and general strengths and weaknesses of the company's overall communications. One finding indicated that employees want more information about the company's strategic planning, goals and relationship to its communities.[6]

What appears to be taking place is that management is listening to employees and involving them in the real decisions facing the organization. Internal corporate communication lines, newsletters, magazines, written media, and face-to-face exchanges now deal with substantive issues rather than chatter about births, bowling leagues, promotions, and pending retirements. Foltz feels that "internal public affairs, along with public affairs generally, is moving to the bottom line. Internal subjects being addressed are productivity management, quality circles, health care cost containment, union prevention and decertification, absenteeism and competition."[7]

The reason behind promoting employee interest in internal corporate communications is mainly to motivate employees to participate and to meet some of the challenges facing the manager of the future. Business counselor David Johnston offers these guidelines for observing internal communication efforts.

1. Encourage face-to-face dialogue between and across employee levels. Publications and audiovisual tools should supplement, not replace, interpersonal communication.

2. Target communications to major employee subgroups.

3. Tailor messages to help employees better understand their jobs, the company's mission, and the personal and corporate citizenship role.

4. Encourage employees to make suggestions.

5. Senior management should remain accessible.[8]

The Perspective of the Chief Executive Officer

According to a recent survey of corporate chief executive officers by the International Association of Business Communications, "In terms of corporate priorities, the vast majority of [chief executive officers] rated employee communication in the extremely important, very important, or tops categories."

A sampling of chief executive officer responses shows their concern:

"There is a direct correlation between employee communication and profitability."

"The success or failure of everything from new products to advertising campaigns to reaching our goals for the fiscal year are affected by how well our employees understand what we are trying to accomplish and how we accomplish it."

"If employees understand what you're trying to do and get involved in the process feeling like they're really a part of it, then the job gets done more easily, and there are fewer grievances and fewer problems.[9]

Successful internal communication must be a shared responsibility. Managers must be concerned and employees must take the challenge to participate actively in decision making, not just in times of crisis, but on an ongoing basis. Successful communication policy can be built on management's desire to:

1. Inform employees of organizational goals, objectives, and plans.

2. Inform employees of organizational activities, problems, and accomplishments.

3. Encourage employees to provide input, information, and feedback to management based on their experience, insights, feelings, creativity, and reason.

4. Level with employees about negative, sensitive, or controversial issues.

5. Encourage frequent, honest, job-related, two-way communication among managers and their subordinates.

6. Communicate important events and decisions as quickly as possible to all employees.

7. Establish a climate where innovation and creativity are encouraged.

8. Have every manager and supervisor discuss with subordinates their progress and position in the firm.

THE MEDIA OF EMPLOYEE COMMUNICATION

Employee communication programs use all media as means of conveying information. The flow runs upward and downward and across all employee levels. Interpersonal channels range from face-to-face exchanges to corporate shareholder meetings. With greater frequency, media with limited human access are used in the total communication strategy. Managers and supervisors, working primarily through one-on-one and small group communications, remain the most critical communications line. These efforts are supplemented with small and large meetings, letters, periodicals, newsletters, exhibits, annual reports, handbooks, manuals, envelope stuffers, and reading racks. To reach more employees quickly, closed-circuit television, telephone hot lines, surveys, suggestion systems, films, and combinations of these are used in total communication efforts. These media, and their combined communications, carry the corporate image.

Carrying the corporate image to employees requires an endless effort to explain benefits, vacations, holidays, taxes, workers' compensation, affirmative action, and equal employment opportunity policies. Employees can be informed of community issues and educational and training opportunites. Other image objectives include encouraging employee advancement, demonstrating the organization's concern for workers' health and safety, and interpreting local, state, and national news as it applies to the company and well-being of employees.

Internal communication should promote the idea that each employee is a salesman for the company, building loyalty to the organization, improving cooperation and production, and promoting efficiency in an effort to reduce expense and waste.

The House Organ—Company Newsletters

Printed communication must take its place as a part of an overall program including interpersonal communication and public exposure of corporate officials, all within the context of establishing appropriate climate and policy.

More than 50,000 in-house publications in the United States circulate to more than 460 million workers. Large organizations find it useful to have more than one publication. For instance, a newsletter may be directed toward a single employee function or level, such as sales, managers, or chief executive officers. One automaker, because of its size and the variety of its audiences, publishes thirty-eight in-house newsletters. These are ordinarily intended for internal distribution and not for the general public. Occasionally, however, they are distributed to influential people outside the organization or even used as marketing tools.

One broad goal of an in-house publication is to improve relations between employee readers and management. The house organ must fill the needs of both the organization and its employees. Content should combine the interests of management and employees and it should chart and promote the corporate image. For example, recognizing employee achievements—both on the job and in the community—encourages internal cooperation and helps management and employees become better acquainted.

The house organ serves as official ambassador promoting goodwill among employees. Employee recognition promotes the objectives of building a sense of accomplishment in individual employees, stimulating new ideas for company and community services, and strengthening a positive relationship with the outside community. From management's point of view, the ambassadorial role should increase support for management. Clarifying management policies builds confidence in management while helping combat rumors and misunderstandings.

Other Print Media

The in-house newsletter should be reinforced by other written channels that promote corporate image. Booklets and manuals, for example, explain the company insurance package, company retirement programs, and other benefits. They also review social and community issues in which the company is involved.

Most large corporations maintain corporate libraries that serve as a reservoir for manuals, training materials, videotapes, films, reports, new-employee information, and as a central resource center for a business book collection. If printing expenses are prohibitive, limited copies of booklets and manuals are best made available in the company library. Company libraries afford employees direct access to resources not found in the home or community library. The corporate library boosts the corporate image by showing employees that the organization is willing to invest in its most important asset, the people who make up the corporate family.

One especially useful booklet is the new-employee orientation manual. Orientation literature starts new employees in the right direction by setting ground rules and by explaining company goals, philosophies, and objectives.

Leaflets, inserts, and enclosures are another practical form of print media. An insert in a pay envelope allows an immediate problem to be addressed in short time, setting the record straight and squelching distasteful rumors.

Message displays are means of reaching large numbers of people quickly and inexpensively. These channels include posters, billboards, bulletin boards, information racks, and exhibits. These media should be packaged and repackaged to keep them up-to-date and interesting. Posting certain information is required by law. Another important image consideration is that these media supplement or follow-up announcements can be made in meetings or in the company newsletter. Image themes such as showing how a production facility works or depicting the history of the business are more interesting when conveyed visually.

Interpersonal Channels

Question-and-answer sessions between managers and employees close the distance between managers and subordinates and show that managers are real people with human concerns. These sessions demonstrate that the boss is open to communication and they provide an excellent opportunity to correct misunderstandings and deal firsthand with substantive issues. They become excellent means for venting minor irritants, praising employees for a job well done, analyzing why a project increased productivity, or discussing why the profit margin is slipping. Sessions may be confined to a specific topic or issue, or they may include a variety of subjects.

Committee meetings show that managers welcome input from employees. Combining employee and management teams to handle problems relays the message that committees and teams are representative of the people and it promotes cooperation among all employee levels.

Informal conversations around the watercooler or over coffee are excellent one-to-one communication tools. Many managers make it a point to be available when employees are taking a coffee break to show that they are approachable and that they invite communication. Grapevine networks do exist and office politics are played out in these informal settings. Informal conversations during coffee breaks provide the perfect chance to correct misinformation in the gossip mill.

Social affairs such as receptions, dinners, and parties become an excellent means for building the corporate image. The saying floats around Washington that more business is accomplished in one cocktail party than is accomplished in the office all day. These events become a means for building the name and reputation of a business and for meeting potential clients. A word of caution, however. Company-sponsored social events often garner media attention, and although this can work to your advantage, too many parties decrease credibility because others view the corporation as lax. Executives should avoid excessive socializing. The annual Christmas party appears to be the one time when socializing is appropriate, providing employees a chance to relax and meet in an informal setting.

Luncheon speakers coupled with employee exchanges alleviate employees' perception of a one-sided, top-heavy management organization. An outside speaker can present a situation in a manner that brings perspective and reason to the issue, whereas forcing employees to accept a position heavily promoted by management can backfire if the attempt is interpreted as management dictum. In this case, the likely employee reaction will be increased hostility and further rejection of the issue. Instituting a new policy, especially if employee opposition is strong, can be tempered when a respected outside expert introduces the alien idea. An outsider's opinion, whether accepted or contested, may produce fewer waves, and inside management does not bear the brunt of hostility. Immediate employee feedback and expressed concerns provide insights into employee reactions to controversial issues. Inviting an outside speaker and holding a discussion period provides the spontaneity many employees appreciate in order to express their views. As a result, employees feel they have been consulted about new policies rather than ignored during decision-making.

Training and employee-education funds are gestures that show the company cares about employees and is willing to reward personal initiative. In exchange, employees gain skills that make them better qualified for promotions. Companies might adopt elaborate training and education formats such as that held in-house at the Xerox training facilities near Leesburg, Virginia. Others hire training specialists to provide in-house programs. Still others extend full or partial reimbursement for credit courses, seminars, or other training which employees complete on their own. Advantages to encouraging further education among employees are numerous. Employees build relationships with respected experts, authorities, and community leaders. They form links to professionals with similar problems and interests. Finally, they bring to their jobs improved skills, problem-solving techniques, and conceptual learning, all of which carry over into the workplace.

Other Channels

Stock options allow employee ownership. Employees are more likely to work productively if they feel they own a piece of the action. They become more concerned about profit, more interested in taking part in decision making, and more apt to carry their enthusiasm to family and friends. Many employees are willing to accept less salary if offered a stock option plan.

Employee surveys invite feedback, but obtaining feedback is not enough. To support the survey and the corporate image, results must be analyzed and distributed to employees. Surveys range from suggestion boxes to formal, extensive formats conducted by an outside polling house. Large surveys conducted by companies like Mobil and ARCO not only show interest in employees, but their published results garner a favorable opinion in the eyes of other corporate publics as well.

Objectivity in a survey is paramount and the help of an expert may be a good idea. The phrasing of questions can influence the response or elicit the wrong response. For example, questions cannot simply reiterate management philosophy. On the other side of the coin, employee concerns cannot be supported to the point of exploiting existing hostility. Finally, as survey results are tallied, they must be carefully interpreted. If statistics are misinterpreted or irrelevant, the result is to misinform the public.

Employee videotapes and films become morale builders to instill corporate-family atmosphere, to increase employee awareness, to combat indifference, and to avoid giving employees the feeling they don't count. These media are also used to educate employees about procedures for handling emergencies or consumer complaints.

Aetna Life and Casualty Company developed an employee Consumer Awareness Program (CAP) which encompasses many of the concepts discussed here. In a memo introducing CAP to top management, Philip Roberts, vice president of corporate communications, wrote, "Public perception of our business is, to a large extent, dependent not just on the service provided but the way in which it is performed."[10]

A CAP videotape is shown to home and field office employees who deal with the public. It emphasizes the importance of oral and written communication, and of treating the customer with courtesy—a priority because in the insurance industry the product is the result of crisis. A discussion guide designed to help department managers or supervisors lead informal give-and-take sessions with employees accompanies the videotape. Sample questions in the guide encourage employee response and stimulate dialogue. An employee newsletter, *Aetnasphere*, keeps the program momentum going as the newsletter asks employees to share their customer-relations experiences, both good and bad, and describe what they are doing to improve these relations. Case histories are printed along with the employee's photo. To encourage participation, "Mother Aetna Awards" are presented to those who submit stories.

CAP is successful, as witnessed by the decline in the number of service-related complaints. Complaints declined 28 percent in 1981, according to Aetna, and the company also reports positive feedback from managers.

The program is still in use in the majority of Aetna's 200 field offices for employee communication training, especially for new hires. And CAP led to development of a more extensive training course, part of the company's education cirriculum, for employees who maintain public contact.

Alongside videotapes and films, Aetna utilizes closed-circuit television. This medium allows messages from corporate leaders to be presented to large groups during lunch or other free time. Often, tapes are played that visually explain a product the company manufactures or a service it provides. Television monitors are placed in convenient, high-traffic areas such as lobbies, waiting rooms and lunch rooms, or in outer offices. Videotapes address corporate employees directly, highlighting their diversity and achievements. Videotaped talks by corporate leaders are played for employees to see firsthand the direction management is steering or to become aware of business issues. This is especially important for the multinational corporation, whose business endeavors are complex and varied.

Visitors can take advantage of learning about corporate history or the organizational structure while waiting for appointments. Video presentations intended for visitors cover such topics as how the company is meeting its social responsibility role in the community or how the company contributes to local, state, and national economies.

Company intercoms are also used to build employee morale. Regular motivational messages can be heard by sales staffs who need renewed motivation.

High employee morale is seen by consumers and the community as a positive sign that a company strives for quality—not only in its products and services, but in its internal organization. Because employees become direct broadcasters of internal conflict or content, improved internal relations translates directly into improved corporate image.

NOTES

1. Kristin von Kreisler-Bomben, "Consider the Source," *Continental* (March 1984): 46–53.

2. Roy G. Foltz, "Internal Public Affairs," *The Public Affairs Handbook* (New York: AMACOM, 1982), pp. 249–257.

3. Craig E. Aranoff and Otis W. Baskin, *Public Relations: The Profession and the Practice* (St. Paul, Minn.: West Publishing Co., 1983), p. 201.

4. David C.-H. Johnson, "Communicating Your Company's Social Role," *Public Relations Journal* 4 (December 1981): 18–19.

5. Aranoff and Baskin, p. 198.

6. Ibid., p. 19.

7. Foltz, p. 251.

8. Johnston, p. 19.

9. Louis C. Williams, "What 50 Presidents and Chief Executive Officers Think About Employee Communication," *Journal of Organizational Communication* (Fall 1978).

10. Peg Dardenne, "Mother Aetna to the rescue," *Public Relations Journal* (August 1982): 34–36.

9

Building Community Relations

The image of business so dominates cities, towns, and local communities that we frequently associate those places with local industry. Pittsburgh is a steel town; Washington, D.C., is the seat of government and the center of world power; New York City is the center of world commerce; Houston is an oil town; Los Angeles is associated with motion pictures and television; Detroit means cars.

The close alliance of business and community is even more crucial in small towns where the economic and social lifeblood centers on local corporations. Newport News, Virginia, depends on shipbuilding and shipping. Buffalo, New York, depends on steel and automobile supply manufacturing. Numerous towns, such as small coastal beach resorts, exist for tourism or as retirement communities. If business prospers, the community prospers. If business wanes, the community suffers. During the recent recession, newspaper accounts reported the ruin of entire communities due to company shutdowns.

Other institutions figure into the image mix. Schools, churches, local and state governments, and ultimately the family, all develop an interdependency with local business to guarantee community survival. Institutions guard against infringing on mutual turf. An example is the cancellation of a traditional spring concert scheduled for the campus of American University in Washington, D.C. The vice provost for student affairs, aided by student leaders, canceled the concert because immense crowds were expected. They feared that to deluge the surrounding affluent neighborhood with cars would damage the university's relations with its neighbors. In a similar issue, the university plans a convocation sports center requiring a zoning change. Since neighborhood boards rule on such changes, they are sensitive to the opinions of local groups. Consequently, university officials were careful not to jeopardize the new facility by angering nearby property owners.

Effective community relations depend on the recognition of the interdependence of institutions. Social observer George Sawyer maintains that the key elements for business management in establishing a social balance with the local community are to recognize ways in which business impacts upon the community, and to recognize the basic business/community interdependence.[1]

Business, the local corporation especially, must assume the role of leader in defining, establishing, and implementing the activities among institutions. In the past, constructive community relations programs were characterized as corporate citizens and good neighbors. These terms still have meaning, but they oversimplify the complex relationship between a corporation and the community. During the last fifteen years attention to water and air pollution, elimination of substandard housing, equal opportunity employment and training, local government regulations, and stimulation of minority businesses have formed the basis for greater business involvement in community affairs. These influences necessitate a shift in emphasis on communications programs among business and local community institutions. The image of business now includes social, environmental, and welfare concerns in addition to economic survival.

Community relations activities are as diverse as the communities in which businesses are based. Every business has a vital stake in the health and prosperity of the community it inhabits. The relationship offers rewards on both sides. To the community, business prosperity means employment, wages, a tax base, support of community institutions and activities, and economic stability. Businesses often lend attractive buildings and landscaping to communities, creating an attractive appearance that enhances hometown pride. To the business, a community can offer a skilled labor supply, good living conditions for employees, adequate municipal services, fair taxation, and support for the physical plant and its products.

CORPORATE CITIZENSHIP

Part of the image expected of corporations centers around their willingness to respond to the human needs and interests of the community. Communities, the backbone of towns and cities, face social problems like inadequate housing, proper education, mass transportation, crime prevention and control, street and highway maintenance, minority concerns, unemployment, and other problems inherent in emerging and changing societies. Business has been charged with the responsibility of guiding social change and answering to human needs. Lack of concern quickly tarnishes the corporate image.

Efforts to strengthen the corporate image include building better communities. Informing the community about the organization's products, services, and practices safeguards against misperceptions. The organization must strive to reply to criticism while gaining favorable community opinion and support. Business, on the one side, must know the needs and expectations of the community. On the other side of the coin, the community looks at organizational needs, resources, and expertise. A business organization must plan active, continuous participation with and within a community to maintain and enhance its image to the benefit of both the company and the community.

Image Communication Channels

The corporation uses diverse channels to communicate its image to the community. The channels engaged by an international corporation differ from those of a small, local business. But no matter how large or small or how many locations a corporation has, building a sound corporate image within a community requires preliminary groundwork.

Community relations begin with a clear understanding of management's obligations to the community. This is necessary to coordinate communications and concentrate corporate effort. To determine obligations to the community, corporate management must know the makeup of the community. Demographic, historic, geographic, economic, and other background information which profiles a community is essential. Questions like these must be answered:

1. How is the community structured?
   a. Is the population homogeneous or heterogeneous?
   b. Who are its formal and informal leaders? local government officials? members of the city council and Chamber of Commerce? churches, schools, and civic organization leaders?
   c. Can prevailing value structures be identified?
   d. What communication channels are already in place? Does the city publish a newspaper or magazine? Is word of mouth a main channel? Does the town have a radio or television station? Are communication channels less formal and more personal? For example, are church newsletters, town meetings, or the rumor mill primary information sources?
2. What are the community's strengths and weaknesses?
   a. Does the community face unique sets of problems? For example, is there only one water supply? Has one person dominated the power too long?
   b. What forms the base of local economics? Is your company the base?
   c. Who wields power in the local political scene? What is the political structure and who are the important connections?
   d. What are the unique cultural and natural resources?
3. What does the community already know about your company?
   a. What is the level of understanding of company products, services, practices, and policies?

b. Can you gauge the community's true feelings about your organization?

c. Has the community/corporation experienced misunderstanding in the past?

d. What does the community expect from your corporation?

Answers to these questions are not always obvious. The business/community climate changes and will require constant monitoring and reevaluation. If your corporation is large, you may decide to hire a survey or polling organization to measure prevailing attitudes and perceptions.

Guidelines for Community Relations

The following pointers provide a starting place for developing and promoting productive community relations.

1. Review your organization's policies, practices, and procedures. Are they consistent with sound community relations?

2. Consider especially the following areas: waste disposal; employee recruitment; employment policies (layoffs, compensation, overtime); noise or traffic problems; maintenance of facilities and grounds; advertising, signs, and marketing; energy sources and energy waste.

3. Develop specific community relations objectives. Base policy on assessment of organizational needs, resources, and expertise, and on community needs and expectations. Such objectives might include attracting women and minority employment applicants; improving community awareness of company contributions; improving relations with local government; improving local school systems to make the community more attractive to potential executives and professional employees; and improving the quality of local colleges.

4. Use various channels to communicate with the community. Channels may include employees, local media, open houses, local clubs and organizations, local advertising, direct mail, newsletters, brochures, annual reports, films, and exhibits.

5. Involve your company leaders in local organizations. This may be accomplished by sponsoring employees who join civic and professional groups; providing speakers for meetings; lending facilities for meetings or other activities; sponsoring contests and youth programs; and supporting fund-raising activities.

6. Offer aid to local governments. Make company resources of employee time and expertise as well as materials available to local governments.

7. Patronize local merchants, banks, insurance agencies, lawyers, and other local businesses.

8. Distribute corporate donations according to community relations policies and objectives.

9. Evaluate community relations efforts frequently. Measure the extent to which

objectives are being met. Be prepared to modify old or develop new strategies.

ACTIVE MANAGEMENT INVOLVEMENT

Far more important than impersonal channels is management's direct involvement with community leaders. Taking an active role requires establishing a rapport and open association with opinion leaders. Seeking the favorable opinion of leaders who guide the community is a logical first step. Among these leaders are public officials, professionals, and executives from other companies. Ethnic and neighborhood leaders, union leaders, clergy, teachers, and professors are among other groups who should not be overlooked when promoting community relations.

Managers meet community leaders by joining local organizations. Much is accomplished in face-to-face meetings where discussions of common concerns like rezoning or toxic waste control take place. Panels whose makeup includes representatives from business, local government, and media provide personal exchanges. Opening panels to the public provides a forum to discuss issues and solve problems. These forums may be televised by a cable channel to broaden the audience exposure. Audiences, composed of local community members, exchange ideas during question-and-answer sessions. Telephone call-ins further allow radio listeners or television viewers to participate in the exchange.

The corporate image is enhanced if managers become involved in civic, service, fraternal, and social organizations. Active involvement affords managers a chance for direct input into these groups. Membership in the local Chamber of Commerce provides easy access to information about the community. Rotarians, Elks, and myriads of similar professional and public service groups are alternatives which build the corporate image.

Involvement in local political events enhances the manager's image as well as the image of the company. National political parties maintain local clubs that provide direct access to community, county, and state government leaders.

Employee volunteer programs become a prime channel to enhance the corporate image. Volunteer activities may be as simple as coaching a little league softball team, or as complex as a corporate-wide speakers bureau or volunteer network. A volunteer service program gives employees an opportunity to help others and to experience personal growth while getting to know people in the community. Employee morale and attitudes toward the company receive a lift and a direct benefit in that organizations see firsthand that the company is concerned. ARCO's Volunteer Service Program involves over 1,000 employees in programs for the elderly and teenagers, for the mentally handicapped, and for consumer education, public transportation, and health care.

The exemplary work of Linda Maccione, Denver employee and recipient of ARCO's Community Service Award, is proof of corporate support of employee good deeds. Maccione works with Sacred Heart House, an association that provides emergency shelter and assistance to single women and families. In charge of the Wednesday night shift, Maccione admits guests, answers phones, and supervises meals. She also acts as a job counselor, offering suggestions on job placement. ARCO showed its appreciation to Linda by contributing $500 to her favorite charity in her name, plus a personal gift of a Tiffany desk clock.

Local Government and Political Action

Corporations, as major taxpayers and users of municipal services, have a great stake in local government. Keeping the corporate image on solid footing requires firm business relations with local governments, governing agencies, and their leaders. The Reagan Administration, attempting to shift responsibilities from the federal and state levels to local governments, has caused corporations to mobilize on the local level. Business leaders are learning to speak out on policies in the best interest of their company and the community. Community relations are integral parts of the national lobbying effort.

ARCO is a proven leader in establishing and maintaining healthy local government and community relations. It has sponsored numerous conferences titled *Partnerships: Public/Private*. The unique partnership, devoted to community progress, allies the U.S. Conference of Mayors and ARCO. To date, over 200 state and local organizations and some 300 government, business, and community leaders nationwide have participated. Executives from the public and private sectors attended a recent collaboration held in Carson, California.

Three national conferences and eighteen months of research have been invested so far in the design of a successful partnership model. The partnership model encompasses: 1) leadership—it emphasizes the need for community leaders, not just from business but also from the civic and nonprofit arenas; and 2) defining stakeholders—through a community audit, it identifies key people who figure into the community's future.

Data resulting from questions concerning citizen social and ethnic backgrounds profile a community, giving a corporation the necessary base on which to form policy. Moreover, these initial steps allow community problems to be addressed individually. Using creative, nontraditional problem-solving techniques, the corporation can identify, prioritize, and categorize problems. Afterwards, an action plan can be developed.

Forum procedures are perhaps less important than the precedent the forum establishes. Conference business and community leaders create a valuable resource that addresses critical problems facing America's communities. These partnerships represent a new direction in community social and material revitalization. These structures, formed with partners who seek resolution of problems for everyone's benefit, serve the entire community.

On the home front, business leaders can increase their involvement by serving on local boards that make decisions affecting the corporation. County and city governments pass resolutions bearing a direct effect on how, and if, a business operates. Representation by business leaders not only safeguards the corporate image, but decisions rendered by local government often determine if a business will continue to exist.

INTEGRATING A BUSINESS INTO A COMMUNITY

A company can bolster its standing and its image when relocating or expanding in a community. Corporate infringement, on the other hand, can result in ill feelings that may take years to repair should the move be mishandled. The community might interpret a move as an invasion that results in a drain on limited resources. Added wastes and sewage are unwelcome and many communities resent increased congestion, traffic, and displacement of rural or farm properties. The community may overlook the economic advantages unless a strategy to integrate the company into the community is handled with care.

Advance planning is a first step. Atlantic Richfield again provides a model. ARCO Transportation transferred some 250 employees to a new headquarters in downtown Long Beach, California. Company managers pondered ways to encourage employees to become involved in the community without generating unrealistic expectations among civic leaders.

Approximately six months prior to the move, ARCO Transportation formed a Community Involvement Council to serve as a clearinghouse for matching ARCO human and financial resources, experience, and expertise with the needs of the community. Employees were prepared by an article in an employee newsletter about the cultural and service groups of Long Beach. A pool of employee and retiree volunteers went to work. Some tutored elementary school children, and sports enthusiasts involved themselves in the Long Beach Volleyball Association.

Other measures taken to oil the transition included gifts to the Long Beach Museum of Art and to the Regional Arts Foundation for a "Jazz at the Beach" series. The Long Beach Symphony Association received a $35,000 grant.

Through active community involvement at a time of community upheaval, ARCO demonstrated that the vitality of a modern corporation is closely linked to the health of the surrounding community.

Other Direct Links

Knowing the community structure and maintaining active management involvement with the community are primary steps to solidify the community/corporate image link. Corporations have begun to embark upon other links to secure their image within the community. Open houses offer the community a firsthand glimpse of business operations. Corporate philanthropy and sponsorships, though sometimes controversial, send a clear image message, not only to the local community, but frequently with national overtones.

Open Houses

Whether a new or established business, opening the corporate doors to the community is a sure means of building corporate image. An open house sends the message of interdependence and signals openness between the corporation and the community. In some cases, business tours grow into major tourist attractions. People flock to taste wine at the California vintners located in Napa and Sonoma counties. Visitors to Puerto Rico sample the goods at rum-producing companies. Visitors to the Philip Morris tobacco company in Richmond, Virginia receive sample packs of cigarettes.

A typical open house includes a tour of the facilities. Knowledgeable guides lead small groups around the physical plant, responding to questions. The tour may include a film, video, or display. To cap off the event, a company usually provides a product sample or memento.

CORPORATE PHILANTHROPY

One of the most controversial yet necessary areas of identity building is corporate charity. Corporations increasingly find themselves beseiged with requests for funds. In recent years as government funding of arts and education has been sliced from the federal budget, targeting corporations for charitable contributions has become commonplace. Yet questions about the motivations and goals of corporate giving are raised. Corporate leaders fear, with good reason, the charge of "influence peddler." Nevertheless, by asking local managers of corporate branches to decide on allocation of charitable funds, large corporations ensure that they are in touch with the needs of local communities. Consequently, corporate donations are becoming a more accepted practice in corporate management.

A corporate-wide policy must be established to determine how funds will be spent, where they come from, who will monitor distribution, and who will receive funds. Corporate executives must establish a policy about charities and determine what form of philanthropy best serves the corporation's long-term self-interest. One factor in making this determination should be the corporate image. Surveys indicate that patterns of corporate giving fit well the doctrine that corporations should provide funds to causes that serve the broadly conceived interests of the firm.

Corporate philosophy on giving should include the following considerations:

1. Criteria for evaluating requests for funds should include the types of organizations to be supported and the method for grants administration. Large organizations establish separate foundations that receive a tax-exempt or other special tax category to evaluate and administer requests for grants. A small organization may wish to work with only one or two groups, such as a symphony, a softball team, or the fire and rescue squad.

2. Communication, especially feedback from recipients, serves to promote favorable corporate image. Reports on amounts given to particular recipients and their use of the funds should be relayed to employees, stockholders, members of the community, and others having a vested interest. Articles in the local newspaper, the employee newsletter, or the annual report should keep these publics updated on philanthropic efforts. If donations affect dividends, keeping stockholders updated is especially important.

Employees who own stock or participate in profit-sharing plans may elect to set aside a percentage of profits for charities. In such cases, they want to know where and how their money is spent. The same holds true for stockholders. Many corporations set aside an amount to be donated and seek stockholder approval. By law, up to 5 percent of earnings may be donated to charitable organizations.

Within the community, business can improve its identity by contributing to educational institutions. Minority education is a prime target. Some businesses elect to bring minority groups in-house and provide on-the-job training with an eye toward permanent hiring. This option gives those who lack skills a chance to improve themselves and move up the corporate ladder. Other businesses elect to establish a college scholarship or support a high school training program such as driver education or a specific group such as Students Against Drunk Driving.

Health projects and welfare institutions become corporate funding targets. Contributions to local heart associations or cancer societies are examples. During holidays employees and managers form teams to raise funds to donate to childrens' homes or homes for senior citizens. If funds are unavailable, gifts of food and clothing may be substituted.

Corporate philanthropy extends beyond financial support. Employee volunteers speak to high-school or college classes or invite students into the business. Paid and nonpaid internships give students firsthand experience in business operations. And school administrators may work in the company for a brief period to strengthen financial or managerial expertise.

Corporate support of the arts is a fast-growing area of corporate funding. Support may extend from lending corporate office space to an artist as a gallery to sponsoring international art exchange programs. Corporations also hire local architects, designers, and artists to guarantee that company buildings and grounds are aesthetically pleasing.

Corporations reach into the community through special fund-raisers. After the burning of Wolf Trap Farm Park, an outdoor, Washington community performing arts center, local companies came to the rescue, donating money, building supplies, and manpower to rebuild it. Companies pledged funds through local television and radio fund-raising programs while company employees manned telephones to handle calls.

Companies sponsor public service television programming. Large corporations like Exxon and Mobil bring opera, ballet, and the symphony to communities that otherwise might not enjoy them. Businesses also sponsor the production of special television programs like the Smithsonian Productions or National Geographic specials. When public broadcast stations hold fund-raisers, company employees donate their time to operate phone banks.

Like anything else, a corporation must adjust to its environment to flourish. If employees are a company's primary public, as pointed out in the preceding chapter, the community is a company's most primary and immediate environment. To thrive, a company must work well within that environment and the community environment must in turn provide a healthy climate for the company. A company which attempts to isolate itself from the surrounding community becomes a focal point of public suspicion and mistrust, both of which could erupt into open hostility at an unforeseen provocation. But a well-developed community relations program goes far toward establishing a company as a community leader and a welcome "citizen."

NOTE

1. George Sawyer, *Business and Society: Managing Corporate Social Impact* (Boston: Houghton Mifflin, 1979).

10

Consumer Concerns

The ARCO/Harris poll shows alarming erosion in how Americans value the quality of products, repairs and services. Almost half the public believes that if you buy a product, it will break down right away, won't work as it should, and if you take it to be repaired, it won't be fixed properly. These views are up considerably over what they were in 1976.

—Virginia H. Knauer,
Special Adviser to the President for Consumer Affairs[1]

Consumer perception of the makers of goods and the providers of services appears at an all-time low. Based on the above-mentioned 1982 study conducted by Louis Harris and sponsored by ARCO, consumer worries are up considerably since 1976. *Consumerism in the Eighties* is the landmark study of the past decade. In fact, assessment of consumerism at national levels is a recent development. The only other significant study, *Consumerism at the Crossroads*, was conducted by Harris and Associates in 1976.[2]

Consumer concerns, according to the 1982 study, center around the poor quality of products, the poor quality of service and repairs, misleading packaging and labeling, companies' failure to handle complaints properly, and inadequate guarantees or warranties. Consumers also think business is offering poor-quality products at high prices, thus giving declining value in the marketplace.

The alarming contradiction about the findings is that American business could be so unconcerned about offering the buying public quality goods and services. Products and services are the most immediate link between a company and the consuming public. The quality product or service reflects the company's image and is tied directly to economic survival. A notable example is the success of Bayer aspirin. Many consumers refuse to buy other brands even at less cost. The image of product quality accounts for the success of the maker. Other great American success stories tie product quality directly to corporate image. IBM microcomputers have survived the competition in large part due to IBM's image not only of selling a quality product but of providing fast repair and service. Marriott Corporation goes a step further than competitors in guaranteeing hotel guests comfortable, clean rooms, and Marriott's fast food chains provide consistently good food. The public image is one of quality, reliability, and value for the money.

Over and over the formula—product quality, customer satisfaction, sound image, and profits—holds true. But too often the expressed support of quality appears to be only lip service. Attitudes such as "Let the buyer beware" or "Do unto others before they do unto you" prevail. Yet some corporations with reputations for dependability do more than simply espouse concern for the buyer.

Giant Food's theme, "Giant offers quality, service and value . . . from the people who care," is a good example. Posted throughout Giant stores, the theme is more than mere words on cardboard. Giant's personnel visit suppliers to ensure that Giant brands are comparable in quality to brand-name products. A quality assurance director visits plants to test quality and inspect facilities. Random tests within Giant further check product quality. These efforts demonstrate to customers that Giant is doing something more and set Giant apart from other food retailers who may sell store-brand products of lesser quality.

A LESSON FOR CORPORATE AMERICA

The lesson corporate America must learn is that consumers' concerns are reflected on two levels. The rise of consumer movements and leaders is the first level. Consumer movements may involve specific groups with specific concerns targeted at one organization. These movements frequently lead to costly product change or reposition, if not to removal of products altogether from the marketplace. Cordless telephones are a recent example. Purchasers of remote telephones have come to realize that their conversations are easily overheard on radio band signals. A national newscast focused on the issue of invasion of privacy and reported that two people had been convicted of drug dealing. It's now up to the courts to determine if privacy was indeed invaded. The repercussion for the producer was a recall of the product with a mandatory warning to consumers.

Responses extend from Ralph Nader and other activist groups to the Consumer Protection Agency and to consumer agencies formed in towns and counties around the country. Many people won't make a major purchase without first consulting the respected publication *Consumer Reports*. Local libraries reserve entire sections for consumer informatiom. Cities publish local consumer guides to rate businesses including dry cleaners, tire suppliers, plumbing services, even restaurants. Fear of buying has become a national concern.

Product Image

The second level of concern is the basic human level. As Thomas Peters and Robert Waterman note in *In Search of Excellence*, "Business success rests on something labeled a sale, which at least momentarily weds company and customer."[3] It's at this basic level that buyers are likely to decide whether they like or dislike a product. Their like or dislike determines the repeat-purchase decision. Odonna Mathews, consumer advisor for Giant Food, underscores the point when she remarks, "Word of mouth is an important measure of success. If a customer is satisfied, he or she will tell four or five people. On the other hand, if they're dissatisfied, they will tell nine or ten people. It doesn't take long for the word to get out."[4]

The link between consumer purchase and product image is considered important enough by some companies that they perform elaborate test marketing. Product appeal, reflected through name, packaging, and labeling, entices customers. Because a negative shelf image fails to stimulate the consumer, test marketing considers the subtleties of shape and color. Attractive, point-of-purchase packages are strategically placed on shelves to tempt the hurried shopper to pick up products and try them.

Once the pruchase is made, the real test is at home. The name and label may provide initial enticement, but sampling the contents is the proof. Such tests provide the impetus for dozens of television ads of harried shoppers testing a laundry detergent and exclaiming over the results, vowing never to buy a competing product. The point may seem overly simple, but it's the heart of the consumer decision to buy and to continue buying.

Consumer Awareness of the Corporate Image

What emerges is a consumer who is aware of products and services, a more educated consumer, and one who is leery of buying from a company with a questionable reputation. Product quality, dependability, and reputation for services figure into the consumer's placing and retaining faith in a business. A company that goes out of its way to build a solid public image must ensure that its reputation reflects quality and dependability. Reversing the buying public's perception of business begins with offering quality, reliable products and services, backed by a sound repair record.

THE CORPORATE RESPONSE

Concern for consumer issues is fast becoming a top management priority. Most corporations respond with a consumer relations, customer service, or communications department. Whatever its name, the work of this department centers around resolving complaints, disseminating consumer information, advising management on consumer issues, and dealing with outside consumer advocate groups.

Many large corporations maintain consumer affairs teams at both the corporate and divisional levels. One common characteristic, regardless of structure and placement, is that the vast majority of consumer affairs units report directly to top management. The structure of a long-distance telephone company includes a vice president of consumer relations, headquartered in the corporate office. Regional managers report directly to him. Complaints from major clients or problem accounts become the direct charge of the vice president and are given priority treatment by him and his staff. Regional offices support the corporate office handling customer queries and complaints.

Consumer relations have become a direct responsibility of management because what the consumer thinks and says directly affects the reputation of the company. Managers must have a handle on consumer feedback to respond appropriately.

Evidence of the importance business places on consumer issues is seen in the willingness of some companies to take action against those who do not respond to consumer concerns. Giant Food has enlisted the assistance of some of its suppliers to label their products and help customers know more about their contents and precautions in use. Should suppliers fail to label Giant products as requested, Giant may drop those suppliers' lines. This action not only places additional pressure on manufacturers who do not comply, but enhances Giant Food's image by reflecting concern for product quality and safety.

Peters and Waterman, authors of the best-seller *In Search of Excellence*, devote a chapter called "Close to the Customer" to customer relations. They maintain that satisfying the customer would naturally seem a high priority item on the corporate agenda. Yet they discovered just the opposite in many cases. "A simple summary of what our research uncovered on the customer attribute is this: The excellent companies really are close to their customers. That's it. Other companies talk about it; the excellent companies do it."

They continue:

In observing the excellent companies, and specifically the way they interact with customers, what we found most striking was the consistent presence of obsession. This characteristically occurred as a seemingly unjustifiable overcommitment to some form of quality, reliability, or service. Being customer-oriented doesn't mean that our excellent companies are slouches when it comes to technological or cost performance. But they do seem to us more driven by their direct orientation to their customers than by technology or by a desire to be the low-cost producer. Take IBM, for example. It is hardly far behind the times, but most observers agree that it hasn't been a technology leader for decades. Its dominance rests on its commitment to service.[5]

STRENGTHENING THE CORPORATE IMAGE WITH CONSUMERS

Consumer relations, like relations with employees and other publics, must be a responsibility assumed by all levels of management. Management must be involved in monitoring consumer complaints in an ongoing effort to stop the problem where it begins and to reinforce the department whose sole responsibility is consumer relations. Many companies have adopted elaborate complaint control systems that include one or more of the following steps:

1. All complaints are logged in immediately upon receipt.
2. As soon as possible after the complaint is received, the complaining party is informed how the problem will be handled.
3. Action on the complaint follows quickly.
4. Departments and personnel affected by the complaint are notified and their responses are monitored.
5. Ongoing analyses are made to determine the pattern of complaints received. This procedure allows preventive action.

The operation of the consumer affairs unit of Chase Manhattan is an example of how such a comprehensive system works. The office monitors complaints, dividing them into about twenty-five categories. Monthly reports are prepared for the entire company and each division. Preventive measures are recommended from these analyses. A summary of typical complaint letters, including direct quotations, is prepared and submitted with the report. Top management finds these summaries particularly revealing and informative. For example, one such analysis revealed that the tone of collection letters issued by the credit department was perceived as irritating. Management reasoned that irritating a customer is not likely to produce payment and only harms the bank's image. Consequently, letters were revised to maintain a firm yet reasonable tone.

Consumer relations departments' structure and means for handling consumer concerns vary with each company. Yet similar threads run throughout companies with effective programs. Dinah Nemeroff of Citibank cites three principal guides: (1) intensive, active involvement on the part of senior management; (2) a remarkable people orientation; and (3) a high intensity of measurement and feedback.

Nemeroff gathered numerous examples of management styles that reinforce the service philosophy. She found that top managers treat service problems as "real time" issues—issues deserving immediate personal attention. She found that top management directly intervenes, ignoring the chain of command, in decisions about service. These managers have frequent regular meetings with junior professionals who respond to customer mail. They pen "marginal notes on customer correspondence" and take immediate action to correct problems.

Nemeroff makes a crucial and surprisingly subtle point concerning another aspect of top management style. She notes that the executives she interviewed "believe they must maintain a long-term view of services as a revenue builder." This point is all too often missed in big American companies. Profit objectives, while necessary, are internally focused and certainly do not inspire consumers. Service objectives, on the other hand, are meaningful. A strong sense of personal accountability even among down-the-line employees is achieved when service objectives are clear. And this is crucial. It is an accomplishment when someone in the field says, as did one of Nemeroff's respondents, "Each of us is the company."[6]

Giant Food consumer advisor Odonna Mathews reinforces the need for commitment from top management and for upward and downward communication. As consumer advisor, she reports directly to the president. This ensures that top corporate decision makers hear directly from customers. Pressing concerns are handled on a daily basis. At weekly meetings between management and the operating departments, consumer complaints are reviewed and issues coming directly from the customer are discussed. Ongoing communication and feedback are stressed from the top down and from the bottom up. An operations advisory committee with a rotating membership studies critical areas. Consumer affirs managers often call customers directly or go directly to a store to talk with cashiers, store managers, and even shoppers to uncover potential problems. Employee questions are further urged in the monthly newsletter *We News*. And company chairman and chief executive officer of Giant Food Israel (Izzy) Cohen, son of one of the founding fathers, answers a column called "Letters to Izzy."

Educating Consumers

Commitment from management must be underlined with a sincere desire to treat the customer fairly, to genuinely care about consumer needs. Company slogans or themes are the outward expression, but actions must extend beyond verbal and exterior symbols. Sims Clothing Chain emphasizes that its best customer is an educated consumer. The buyer who knows quality and takes the time to research prices among distributors recognizes when they are purchasing value.

Giant Food goes to great lengths to educate consumers. Information racks in Giant stores contain brochures and handouts that discuss consumer concerns. One brochure discusses the diet needs of senior citizens. A booklet offering recipes for Seder and other religious occasions appeals to the ethnic customer. Brochures explain why buyers should include poultry, fish, meat, fresh vegetables, and fruits in their diets. A monthly publication, *Thumbs Up*, provides advice on nutrition and lists helpful recipes.

In its efforts to educate the public about nutrition, Giant launched a *Foods for Health* program to communicate health information to consumers "in the supermarket at the point of purchase where food decisions are made." This pilot program, conducted in cooperation with the National Heart, Lung, and Blood Institute (NHLBI), was assessed and the results published early in 1984. Among its most significant results were those concerning increased consumer awareness. The results showed that 73 percent of those responding to a telephone survey had "read" or "noticed" *Foods for Health* literature. Moreover, those who had read the materials outnumbered those who noticed them by more than two to one. The program was apparently welcomed by consumers because 94 percent of regular Giant Food shoppers felt supermarkets should supply nutrition information to their patrons.

According to Mathews,

Foods for Health was successful because it combined the marketing, nutrition education and consumer affairs expertise of Giant Food with the scientific, research and educational expertise of NHLBI. We have continued to build on that experience in our more recent programs such as *Special Diet Alert*.

Giant offers a Consumer Bill of Rights as a reminder to its customers and society. Four of the rights were included in the preamble to the March 1962 consumer message former President John F. Kennedy delivered before Congress. These rights include:

1. The Right to Safety—Products should not damage or harm the user. They should live up to makers' claims.

2. The Right to be Heard—Producers of goods and services should guarantee that consumers' views are given consideration.

3. The Right to Choose—The right to choose among various products must be preserved.

4. The Right to be Informed—The consumer should be given easy access to complete and accurate product information. Keeping consumers informed includes improved product identification; unit pricing; data for control of freshness; nutrition labeling; full disclosure of ingredients (which surpasses government requirements) in food, health, and cosmetic products, and percentage of ingredients.

To these four rights, Giant adds the Right to Service and the Right to Redress. The Right to Redress includes "an unconditional, money-back guarantee on all products."

Giant is a fairly heavy user of sixty-second radio spots which offer consumer tips. Changed every other week, these spots can be heard on most radio stations in the Washington/Baltimore areas where Giant Food stores are located.

Many stores communicate directly with consumer advocates and consumer boards. To clarify the role between consumers and management, many companies establish the office of the ombudsman. The primary duties of this person are to carry consumer complaints to management and to seek balance between the customer, the demands of consumer activists, and the goals of the organization. This person must do more than echo the company theme. He or she must remain dedicated to helping senior managers stay in touch with the public.

Many organizations have established panel discussions or a speakers bureau to gain further contact with consumers. Company managers demonstrate concern by participating in these activities. An excellent means of community involvement, these forums allow direct communication with those involved. Corporations have a chance to get their side of the story told to consumers and to the community at large by participating in these types of programs.

Training Employees to Deal with Customers

Employee training in customer service is important to maintain healthy consumer relations. One of the best known examples of such efforts is Disney Corporation's efforts to train employees as family members who entertain. Employees are thoroughly coached about every aspect of creating an atmosphere in which the paying guest is entertained and made comfortable. Training programs teach the principles of dealing with the public, public speaking, working in groups, and developing interpersonal communication and telephone manners.

Quality circles and the president's gold club are ideas replicated in one form or another in many companies. Employees with outstanding customer service records are singled out for special recognition. In a typical arrangement, managers monitor employees whose outstanding handling of consumer complaints offers guidelines for overcoming difficult problems. Employees from various departments are nominated, finalists chosen, and one person selected for an award, such as a vacation, bonus, or other special treatment. These events signal to employees that the company cares about them and is aware of how important they are in promoting customer/company relations.

Employees and customers are often perceived as reflections of each other and certainly as primary publics of concern to the business. Satisfied employees spread high morale throughout the company and to all they come in contact with, including the customer. The customer senses this employee contentment. Giant consumer advisor Mathews points out that much of the image formed by the customer is based on the friendliness and helpfulness of employees. What the customer experiences in the store becomes the customer's lasting impression of the company.

In an age when computer transactions, computer-generated mail, and impersonal service reign, two-way personal contact—the human touch—appears to be at the core of sound consumer relations. Handwritten notes are again in vogue, possibly to offset the word-processed message. This concern for treating the customer fairly and directly and the desire to offer quality and service go a long way toward turning negative public images into positive ones.

CONSUMER PROFILE

Consumer concern is strong and growing. A new kind of social and political force that does not follow traditional battle lines in American society is causing consumerism to break traditional molds. Telephone interviews conducted for *Consumerism in the Eighties* from October 15 to 26, 1982, included randomly selected adults from across the United States. From the survey it was learned just how far the break from traditional consumerism has come.

Upper-income and higher-education groups are more consumer-oriented than people with lower incomes and less education. Women are often more proconsumerist than men. And political independents and ideological middle-of-the-roaders are proconsumerist. Groups with the most consistently proconsumerist tendencies also include the young, individuals living in or near cities, Blacks, self-described liberals, and Democrats. Groups with the least consistently proconsumerist tendencies include town and rural dwellers, the older generation, Whites, self-described conservatives, and Republicans. Nevertheless, the newer group differences overlay these traditional patterns and restructure the resulting coalitions. These patterns represent a dramatic change from coalitions dating from the New Deal days. The findings suggest that consumerism cuts across traditional social and political barriers and produces new or modified kinds of coalitions.

According to the study, Blacks, females, and senior citizens are emerging consumer groups with clout. The overall picture of Black consumers that emerges from these figures is a group that seems particularly vulnerable to consumer problems. They become allies of those who press for more government regulation and who endorse the achievements of the consumer movement and its leaders in the past, but they do not feel well served by the movement today. Potential support for the movement is strong in the Black community.

Women are more likely than men to worry about consumer concerns and they are less likely than men to see progress in the marketplace. The picture of women consumers that emerges from the survey differs only occasionally from that of their male counterparts. This is not too surprising, since men and women spend much of their lives sharing households or family units and thus experience similar consumer environments. One might expect the objective consumer environment and the subjective consumer experience to differ more by indices such as place of residence, income bracket, race, or age than by sex.

Nonetheless, women appear more sensitive to consumer problems and less satisfied when these problems remain unresolved. Women seem more likely to think government should do more to protect consumers, and they are slightly more willing than men to pay extra for consumer advocacy.

The picture of senior citizens that emerges from the data is that of a group with a certain skepticism. They seem less convinced than younger people that there has been progress in the marketplace, that the impact of the consumer movement is good, that government regulation is desirable, and that the benefits of consumerism are worth the cost. Accordingly, they are less willing to join, support, or pay for efforts along these lines.

To some extent this skepticism may reflect the natural perspective of a generation brought up in an era when consumerism was not so important or so visible an issue on the national agenda. If so, the senior citizen also might be expected to have reservations about other issues or movements that likewise have emerged only recently.

These findings underscore the conclusion that while consumerism is an issue that draws on traditional political camps, it also cuts across those older divisions and draws people together into new coalitions. In particular, consumerism draws support from higher-income, better-educated people, and independents and middle-of-the-roaders to a degree that distinguishes it as a new kind of social and political movement.

Other highlights from *Consumerism in the Eighties* include the following:

- Public concern about product quality and repair service is growing, not diminishing. Concern about high prices remains top on the list of public concerns.
- Although consumers criticize consumer leaders for being "out of touch" with consumers, they still rate overall consumer movements highly.
- Although consumers realize consumer protection practices raise prices, they believe the price is worth it.
- Many consumers, although not directly involved in consumer movements at present, would become involved under certain conditions.
- Most consumers (two-thirds) believe the Reagan Administration does little to protect consumer interests, and they rate Congress even lower.
- While the Consumer Product Safety Commission receives positive ratings from consumers, the Environmental Protection Agency and the Federal Trade Commission do not. The Consumers Union of the United States, Inc., which publishes *Consumer Reports*, tops a list of eleven agencies involved in protecting consumers.
- Although consumers still feel the need for government regulation of business in specific areas, they feel less need for government regulation in general.
- Consumers view government regulation as necessary when safety and protection are concerned, but consumers are far less apt to endorse government intervention in economic matters.
- Few consumers want less protective government regulation than what is now in place.
- Most consumers want increased government intervention in cases of false advertising.
- Consumers would like to see credit card users pay more to cover credit card costs, and cash-paying customers pay less.
- Consumers are concerned about high interest rates on credit.

If nothing else, these and other findings published in the report demonstrate that consumers are aware, perhaps more than ever before, of what is going on in the marketplace. Besides being more aware, however, they are also more willing to complain. Consumers are coming to realize they have clout either individually or in groups and that they can bring entire corporations to their knees, if necessary, to get the satisfaction they demand.

CORPORATE RESPONSIBILITY TO CONSUMERS

Corporations cannot dismiss the demands of consumers, calling them inconsequential, unreasonable, or unrealistic. A few years ago, no one would have believed packaging of an entire industry such as pharmaceuticals could be radically changed in a short time. Yet after the Tylenol crisis, public clamor produced safer packaging in a matter of only a few months. The public is aware and it demands attention.

And the adhesive which makes possible publics as diverse as Hispanics in the Southwest, businessmen in Chicago, housewives on Nebraska farms, and the retired senior citizen tending his garden, is the media. These groups are aware because they are united by media coverage of consumer concerns.

For this reason, it becomes obvious that a corporation cannot afford to allow the image that reaches these various people to become tainted. If all other publics are important to corporations, the most crucial one is consumers. Corporations must keep their trust by offering quality products and services and they must maintain a corporate image which provides the underlying philosophy which shows they care about consumers.

NOTES

1. Myrlie Evers, "Consumerism in the Eighties," *Public Relations Journal* 39 (August 1983): 24–26.

2. *Consumerism in the Eighties*, A National Survey of Attitudes Toward the Consumer Movement Conducted for Atlantic Richfield Company by Louis Harris and Associates, Inc. (Los Angeles: Louis Harris and Associates and Atlantic Richfield Company, 1983).

3. Thomas Peters and Robert Waterman, *In Search of Excellence* (New York: Harper & Row, 1982), p. 181.

4. Interview materials from Giant Food were supplied by Odonna Mathews, consumer advisor. A special word of gratitude to Ms. Mathews and Giant Food management for providing materials for this book.

5. Peters and Waterman, *In Search of Excellence*, p. 157.

6. Dinah Nemeroff, "Service Delivery Practices and Issues in Leading Consumer Service Businesses: A Report to Participating Companies" (New York: Citibank, April 1980).

11

Government/Business Relations

The direct and indirect influence of government action on business changes
the kinds and mix of skills that one needs to succeed as a manager. Top
managers must now be as concerned about public policy as they are about
anything else they do.

—Grover Starling,
Changing Environment of Business
(Boston: Kent Publishing Co.)

Few days go by without a newspaper or a newscast headline mentioning
a wrangle between business and government. Today's government is a
variable that helps determine business's success or failure. And that is
why business is taking an active role in governmental affairs. That role,
however, is creating public opinion problems for business because industry is being perceived by the general public as an influence buyer.
Business, the public thinks, is trying to purchase government favors. The
creation of political action committees (PACs) in 1974, contrary to the
intent of the legislation that produced them, has fed this public perception. PACs were formed in an attempt to stop influence buying. Yet their
perceived purpose remains evil in the public's eye.

During the early 1984 presidential primaries, Walter Mondale felt the
heat of the public's burning belief that PAC contributions are influence
chips in the political poker game. After he received nearly $500,000 from
labor groups, the belief that Mondale was becoming their pawn grew so
strong that he was forced to return the money. Return the money, that
is, or risk losing votes to his opponent Gary Hart, who cleverly asked
the public through television commercials, "Can a president act in our
national interest when he owes so much to special interests?"[1]

In situations like this, the public sees business and government as allies working for their own benefit and ignoring the goals of public welfare. In reality, quite the opposite picture exists. Government and business rarely work together. In fact, they usually work against one another. Government attempts to regulate business and business attempts to limit government regulation.

Neither the perceived image of business and government as allies nor the more accurate picture of business and government as adversaries is good for maintaining a positive corporate image. Today a corporation must exert pressure on government to stay afloat, but it does not have to purchase power with PAC gifts. The necessary pressure can be exerted by working with government to find solutions to problems that can be both profitable for business and beneficial to the public at large.

The recent government/industry conferences that attempted to decide what should be done about ethylene dibromide (EDB) pollution exemplify ways government and business can work together. EDB, a cancer-causing fumigant sprayed on stored grain, fruit, and milling equipment, had been found on more than a hundred products on grocery shelves. In addition, according to newspapers, EDB may have tainted nearly all the nation's 7.7 billion bushels of stockpiled grain. This situation not only resulted in a major national incident, but it caused embarrassing international repercussions because 3.7 million tons of corn and wheat possibly containing EDB had already been delivered to the Soviet Union to fulfill part of the agreed sale of 7.1 million tons of products for the year.

At home, Florida recalled seventy-seven common grain-based products, California banned importation of citrus fruit fumigated with EDB, and Texas officials battled over whether or not to halt sales of nineteen food products that were found to contain the chemical. These were decisions and situations too large to be left to business or government discretion alone. Both groups necessarily became involved. And they worked together for the public good, rather than as adversaries.

Unfortunately, situations like this are few and far between. Daily relations between business and government are strained at best. But existing adversarial attitudes should be replaced with a cooperative public/private environment. Efforts must be made to reconcile public interest with the profit motive and to ensure that business and government coexist peacefully. Why? To protect the corporate image.

Public image of corporations rests not solely on a cooperative environment, but on a sound and coordinated program reflecting the corporation's stand on issues mutually affecting both business and the public at large. The Opinion Research Corporation (ORC), through its semiannual Washington Thoughtleaders Surveys, monitors the effectiveness of business communications in Washington. ORC vice president Kenneth Schwartz comments on the results of surveys:

While business has improved the effectiveness of its communications in Washington, individual corporations still have a long way to go. Indeed, thoughtleaders—particularly members of Congress, the executive branch, and the media—believe corporations, collectively and singly, should make themselves more, not less, visible in the nation's capital.[2]

To maintain a coordinated communications program and to be heard as loudly and clearly as possible in Washington, Schwartz recommends avoiding "the hit-or-miss approach" which involves fighting legislation after the fact. What should be sought is constructive business involvement in the development of legislative proposals and in the rule-making procedures of the regulatory agencies, balancing problems and concerns of business with the interest of the public as a whole.

Schwartz continues:

What seems also to be called for is a cohesive, coordinated communications strategy based on corporate positions, established at the highest executive level, on public policy matters. Such positions should be communicated both in writing and through direct personal contact with all of a corporation's key publics—not only in Washington but elsewhere, such as among the media, in the investment community, and among employees and stockholders.[3]

The attitudes of a company's various publics, from the grass roots up, influence the thinking and actions that eventually take place in Washington. Similarly, the actions of individual companies influence the way policymakers view the industry as a whole. Therefore, it is desirable for an entire industry, as well as an individual corporation, to present an integrated and unified communications front in Washington.

Once a corporation has determined its position on a particular public issue, that stance can be expressed in a coordinated manner through activities such as speeches by chief executive officers and other corporate officials, news conferences, press releases, personal interviews with key opinion leaders, articles in plant and employee newspapers and newsletters, management and employee meetings, and personal government contacts in Washington.

A coordinated effort like this guarantees that the company image is molded from one piece of clay and held intact by continual reinforcements. It is left to corporate leaders to ensure that the image statue is built from a well-prepared piece of stone formed with time and care rather than hastily dug from the ground and pounded out in a time of crisis. Situations like the ones created by the handling of EDB and by overzealous PAC contributions create a public perception of a "we-they" conflict—WE the people versus THEY the power brokers and profiteers—that hurts the public images of corporations. The ultimate blame for the evils, regardless of who is at fault, is likely to fall on business

unless an active corporate image campaign is established and a strong
government relations program is created and maintained.

BUSINESS AND GOVERNMENT: OLD FOES

Business/government relations have never been clearly defined. His-
torically, the relationship has been more adversarial than friendly. The
country has moved from a time when business and government retained
a happy friendship to an era in the late nineteenth century when they
became staunch foes. Yet business has recently realized the value of developing a continuing, mutually advantageous relationship with all levels
of government.

Highlights of the often adversarial relationship are noted here to set
the stage for discussion of the means business can employ to improve its
relationship with the government and thus its image with the public at
large. The lesson of the past is that business has become involved with
government only after the fact, reacting only when some critical issue or
legislation forced business to consider the potential harm to its reputation by remaining inert.

Corporations' role in the relationship between business and government was rarely questioned until late in the nineteenth century. Less
regulation of business occurred between 1850 and 1887 than during any
other period of American history. This was the era of business greats
like McCormick, Remington, Westinghouse, Swift, Armour, Pabst, Schlitz,
Duke, and Rockefeller. One sober journalist captured the essence of these
men and of the times when he remarked, "Among the nations of the earth
today, America stands for one idea, BUSINESS, for in this fact lies, potentially, the salvation of the world." And Harper's *New Monthly Magazine* reported, "To the vast majority of Americans, success has long
since come to mean achievement in business and making money."

The image assumed new meaning with the passage of the Interstate
Commerce Act in 1887. The Act marked the beginning of regulatory legislation aimed at curbing monopoly, stopping debilitating business practices, and controlling outright competition. Unions organized in response to abysmal working conditions, strikebreaking, corruption of
corporate and public officials, and monopolistic practices.[4]

Captains of industry came to be known as robber barons. For the first
time in the country, business discovered what it was to be unpopular.
By the turn of the century muckrakers, trustbusters, socialists, and pop-
ulists made business their targets in the courts, in voting booths, and in
the streets. Even so, Woodrow Wilson proclaimed, "Business underlies
everything in our national life." And Calvin Coolidge still claimed, "The
business of America is Business!"

Gradually, a more moderate position emerged which held that while the game was basically good, some of the rules needed modification. In pursuit of economic gain, valid social needs were being overlooked. As a result, legislation was passed in areas including antitrust, labor relations, child labor, food and drug purity, and copyrights. But with each additional statute, government assumed added functions. It became a rulemaker and a referee.[5]

Popular support for business returned to relatively high levels in the 1920s, but it was short-lived. The Depression shook business prestige as well as profits. Bankruptcies, mass unemployment, and economic stagnation engulfed the country, seeming to suggest that the American Dream was counterfeit. When business failed to perform as promised, older values were called into question and new solutions were found. Government, regulating the steam of business, became the engine of the economy. And then government assumed responsibility for stimulating business activities, for directly correcting abuses by business, and for relieving industries in distress.

Franklin D. Roosevelt, considered a socialistic devil in some quarters of the business community, was popularly perceived as a saint because, under his administration, the government broke from its traditional role as facilitator and became a provider. Where once government had sought simply to maintain a society in which individuals could pursue their own goals, it now accepted direct responsibility for providing them sustenance.

The New Deal was the demarcation point between trends in American socioeconomic activity. It separated the culture of the self-regulating economy and its individualistic society from that of the mixed economy and its communal society. The alphabet soup of agencies engendered by New Deal legislation made impersonal government bureaucracy a permanent fixture of American life.

But the belief that the New Deal was a rotten plot foisted on innocent business is a misconception. Both the public and business endured the vagaries of a free market that had to pull itself slowly from the grips of the Depression. By mutual consent, the principle that "the government is best which governs least" was abandoned.

Post–New Deal days saw the institutionalization of the movement that its mentor began. Lyndon Johnson took the ball when he created his Great Society welfare system and the Reagan Administration has expressed its recommendation that local governments regulate their corporate citizens more actively. To some extent, business has realized it can no longer pretend to be above the political fray. It has grown to recognize that its interests, indeed its survival, require political acumen. Government's increased willingness to take an active hand in business management and the enormous power of that hand when activated are further pressures for corporate involvement. In response, business involvement in government issues has shifted from activist to preventive. Traditionally, business has resisted the threat of government regulation and intervention. And in the 1980 election President Reagan made reform of expanding government one of his major platform issues. He intended to reduce what he viewed as government meddling in the affairs of business. As public attitudes toward government become more critical and negative, business success in specific and general government activity seems more likely.

The move from an adversarial relationship to greater cooperation between government and business, a trend likely to gain momentum through the rest of this century, is becoming apparent. When asked to interpret the relationship between business and government and its likely development through the year 2000, Raymond L. Hoewing, vice president of the Public Affairs Council, responds:

Overall, for a variety of reasons, predominantly economic reasons, we will continue to see more cooperation of a non-adversarial form. . . . [B]usiness and government are groping for new ways of relating where they have wrestled previously. Public opinion is also pushing toward improved business and government relations.[6]

Hoewing suggests that cooperation will include tax assistance for corporate research and development activities necessary for pioneering new services and technologies. Thought must be given to new ways of communicating and thinking about where the country is headed. Government and business must cooperate in order to formulate industrial policy, and they must cooperate in long-range planning. To accomplish this, business needs to find ways of communicating with government that are efficient, yet consistent with public policy.

Hoewing acknowledges that businesses are subject to "more self-regulation to alleviate government intervention." He points to the Clean Sites program as a step toward business accepting its responsibility for monitoring itself regarding toxic wastes. He concludes that business must "honestly and religiously try to prevent more government regulation and spending."[7]

Overcoming the Adversarial Relationship

Generally, the public perceives government and business as allied, working for their mutual benefit and forgetting the public interest or ignoring public concerns. Unlike community, consumer, or employee relations, creating corporate image depends upon a noncommitted third party. Often the corporation is at the mercy of a government agency or regulation for which it cannot shape or control the public impact. The impact, in fact, may go directly from the government to the public with the repercussion bouncing back to the corporation, as in the cases of clean air and toxic waste laws. The corporation must bear the brunt of the law, at the same time taking steps to repair the damage its public image suffers.

Corporate leaders, particularly managers, need to look at the job of dealing with government as a complex sequence of acquiring, processing, and disseminating information that impacts upon the corporation and the public at large. Honest and forceful communication between the corporation, the government, and the public becomes crucial to the relations process. The job of the government relations specialist, or lobbyist, provides a good example. On one hand, the specialist must weigh and evaluate issues for their potential impact on the company or industry. The same consideration must be given to the impact issues carry to corporate decision makers, employees, stockholders, and the public at large. On the other hand, their responsibility requires that the same concern be carried from the corporation to legislators, regulators, congressional staffers, political allies, and other key decision makers.

THE CORPORATE/GOVERNMENT COMMUNICATIONS PROGRAM

The corporate/government relations communication program, however, reaches far beyond lobbying. The job begins inside the corporation by educating and involving employees in government advocacy and political issues. It then moves outward to grass roots and federal lobbying, as well as issues management. Positioning of the government relations function varies, but is most likely to be found as part of a department of public affairs or external affairs. Access to top management is a crucial part of positioning. The function must be placed high for people to get answers and responses quickly from top managers on critical issues. Positioning must also allow interaction with key operating and staff positions.

Political Action Committees

At the center of public misperception of business and government relations is the political action committee, commonly referred to as a PAC. At issue is the public accusation that PACs exist to buy every senator, every representative, and every issue in sight. Corporations argue they are only buying one thing—access. The public believes campaign contributions open the door to a legislator's office. This is a misperception based, in large part, upon public misunderstanding of the role a PAC plays in the electoral process. PACs are seen as contributing to candidates' elections, but in reality greater emphasis is placed on working with candidates *after* they are elected. Media stories such as the PAC contributions to the Mondale presidential primary race fuel public misperception.

Public Affairs Council vice president Hoewing cites the following root causes of the controversy over business PACs. (1) PACs are part of the general problem business has in its public image; business PACs are extensions of the overall serious corporate image problem. (2) The public is disenchanted with political campaigns; they run too long and cost too much. Public opinion polls indicate, time after time, that too much money is spent in electing politicians. (3) People are unrealistic about the political process. They view it as a game in which only individuals are involved; they fail to see the need for group involvement. Idealistically, the public condemns PACs because they see the process on the individual level. But realistically, the public should understand the need for groups' interacting in political processes. (4) Public financing of elections is misperceived. Organizations such as Common Cause place demands for accountability on public financing. The public believes elections are bought. And advocacy groups sustain the public perception that PACs influence election outcomes. (5) Media treatment of PACs figures in because issues are dramatized in ways which influence votes. When dollars are mixed with politics, the result is always controversial, and PACs do mix money and politics. Even so, most PAC contributions are given and spent after an election, a fact little known by the general public.

To clear up misunderstandings, the public must be educated about the role PACs play in elections. Hoewing explains, "PACs, collectively, are an overall attempt to get employees involved in government policy affecting the bottom line." Funds for PACs come from employees or stockholders of the business, not from corporate funds at will. To be effective, corporations must first educate their own people and then move outward to the general public. The challenge begins with motivating employees to participate and to decide who is to receive PAC money and why.

Changing the image begins with employee communication channels. Corporations are beginning to use internal newsletters, annual reports, and other written pieces to explain to employees why they should become involved in a PAC. Space is given in the annual report to PAC contributions and support in order to update stockholders on legislative activity. To inform the community and consumers, interpersonal gatherings such as town meetings of local governments are used. A panel representing both the corporation and the PAC recipient comes together to explain their relationship and to answer questions the community may have about the affiliation. Similar gatherings may occur at the state level. For a national or multinational corporation, several pages of the annual report may be given to discussion of PAC involvement and support. Within the corporation, managers and employees alike decide to invite a PAC recipient to meet and to answer questions. Because PAC contributions come largely from employees and stockholders, corporations limit these communication attempts primarily to them. In any communication attempt about PACs, in order to reinforce the corporate image a company must keep in mind that PAC support is perceived as financial involvement. Though the corporation may view PAC giving as part of the policy of enlightened self-interest, consideration must be given to what is good for society as a whole.

Attempts to promote employee and shareholder political awareness are demonstrated by Bliss and Laughlin Industries of Oak Brook, Illinois, which provides worksheets in the envelopes with employees' W-2 forms so they can calculate the percentage of income that goes to taxes and the amount of time each individual must work each year to support the cost of government.

Dow Chemical maintains an extensive public affairs program for employees. It rests on four objectives: (1) informing employees about national and local issues that potentially affect the company; (2) making employees aware of governmental processes and legislative procedures; (3) encouraging employees to take part in the political process and giving examples of specific approaches they can use; and (4) advising employees of the value of political contributions and providing the opportunity for employees to make contributions through PACs.

Budd Company gives its managers a "discretionary bonus" of up to several thousand dollars based on evaluation in several categories, including "involvement in government affairs." Managers are judged on their ability to get people involved in political campaigns, their willingness to write to government officials on issues affecting the company, and their ability to organize in-house PACs. They know that if business intends to remain a viable part of society, its leaders must encourage employee participation in the political process.[8]

Lobbying

A second major influence on the public image of the business/government relationship is lobbying. For years lobbyists have been perceived in the unsavory light of graft and influence peddling. The public thinks lobbyists are simply overpaid lawyers or former government employees who use their influence to gain access to senators, congressmen, and other influential decision makers to secretly write them checks or to give them expensive cars, trips, jewelry, and homes. Abscam and an occasional media exposé showing officials accepting expensive gifts stand as testimony that influence-buying attempts not only happen but are successful. And the public knows that extravagant gifts could not be accepted by government people if they were not offered by business representatives. The corporation and its lobbyists are viewed as the culprits when these situations arise.

In recent years, the public attitude toward lobbying has changed. Lobbyists are now more likely to be perceived as a legitimate and necessary part of business/government relations. The image of influence peddler has gradually shifted to an image of credible business respresentative in Washington or in state capitals. Henry Ford II summed up the new attitude when he remarked, "The problem with 'lobbying' activities is not to conceal their existence, nor to apologize for them, but to make sure they are adequate, effective, and impeccably correct in conduct."[9]

Honesty and credibility are two qualities professional lobbyists strive for in building their careers. As agents acting between business and government, lobbyists must continually work to create a reputation as honest and credible two-way communicators. This reputation reinforces the images of their corporations as honest and credible.

Two-way communication directly links government and business. Lobbyists dig out information from officials, record it, and transmit it to corporate executives. They also attempt to persuasively inform government officials about issues of interest to their companies, to promote or oppose legislation and other governmental actions affecting their company, and to obtain government cooperation for programs their company sponsors. Much of lobbyists' time is devoted to making contacts and creating programs to improve communication with government and to monitor the activities of legislators on statutes and laws. The emphasis in lobbying is on information and advocacy, not pressure. Working through congressional committee staffs or legislative assistants, lobbyists seek to define issues in terms of the legislator's constituency and the public interest.

Public Affairs Council vice president Hoewing suggests that the lobbying function should work in support of public interest. He says people forget that "the political system in this country may be short on a very valuable commodity—information. Congress can't function without information. The lobbyist supplies such needed information." But the public doesn't realize that is what the lobbyist is doing. The corporation must inform and educate the public on these matters as well.

Hoewing also believes lobbyists keep the system honest. "Various interest groups are always trying to undercut each other. Lobbyists, expressing their views, help to get all sides of issues exposed."

This role for the lobbyist is the result of the mass legislation introduced into Congress each session. Congressional staff simply cannot handle the load. Senators and representatives cannot judge the impact of legislation without the input of lobbyists who analyze proposed bills and point out potential consequences.

Lobbyists act as ambassadors of corporate goodwill. As the official spokesperson, the lobbyist carries the corporate image directly to those in power. This role helps educate decision makers and lawmakers about business and economics. Lobbyists also help draft laws and publicize testimony that carries the decision to the corporation's publics, thus gaining favorable or unfavorable opinion for both the corporation and the decision maker.

Many lobbyists form or join a speakers bureau to enhance the corporate image. They address civic, community, educational, or other groups, carrying the corporate reputation with them.

Professional associations support the lobbyists' work and reinforce corporate images through symposiums and education programs. The professional association Women in Government Relations, for example, actively promotes continuous education for its members to ensure that they stay current on important issues, as well as continue to understand the link between government, business, and the public. Their speakers bureau addresses high-school, college, and other audiences to inform people about the lobbyists' job, thus strengthening the corporate image.

The role of the lobbyist is critical in communicating the corporate image. The lobbyist becomes a direct link between the corporation, government representatives, and the public. To support the function, business managers must be willing to keep the lobbyist informed of company policy to be communicated in Washington or to local government and, at the same time, be willing to spread the word on legislative policy to employees. Irene M. Brandt, employed in government relations by Eli Lilly and Company, stresses this role. She has been involved in the field of government affairs during various administrations and congresses.

Brandt states:

The Washington, D.C. process is a continuing process, fundamentally shaped on the dynamics of developing rules collectively for the governing of our society. Because of the dynamics of this process, it is necessary to have an ongoing communication and a networking between the technical expertise of the home office and the government expertise of Washington-based personnel.

This communication occurring regularly improves the sophistication of the home office and the lobbyist to be sensitive to the developing laws and rules and their potential impact.

It is most important for the lobbyist to provide information that is credible and relevant. This is most effectively accomplished by briefings supported by written documents.[10]

Association memberships reinforce the company reputation. Through the association, the company joins and identifies with other companies to focus on long-range goals. Corporations with similar interests form committees to negotiate a position that becomes the industry stance on an issue. The lobbyist may become involved in receptions for members of Congress or joint meetings or seminars with administrative assistants to hash out mutual concerns. These activities go a long way toward improving communication with government while defining issues in terms of both the corporate and public interests.

Grass-Roots Lobbying

If the federal lobbyist is an ambassador in Washington, the corporation and the public at large—grass-roots lobbyists—form the direct link between government and the local business community. Business increasingly seeks to organize employees, stockholders, community leaders, and others as potent weapons in the political decision-making process. This network provides the corporation with the opportunity to carry its image to publics directly affected by the stance the corporation takes on an issue.

The Reagan Administration has placed renewed emphasis on grass-roots lobbying, calling the effort New Federalism. This movement supported the reduction of big government and shifted decision making down to the places it had the greatest impact—at state and local levels. Hoewing notes, "Reagan didn't invent New Federalism; he moved it along. Carter was really making the shift." Hoewing believes the shift will continue. "From the corporate point of view, grass-roots efforts will continue to grow."

Business can use the grass-roots effort to bolster its image by organizing employees, stockholders, community leaders, and voting blocks. Gauging the sentiments of these groups gives the corporation guidelines and feedback to measure its success in living up to public expectations. If these groups express disapproval, the corporation can modify its position. However, support can be generated when needed. For example, the Associated General Contractors of America maintains a legislative network among its 113 chapters across the country. At least one person in each chapter personally knows his senator or representative. This network became instrumental in defeating a labor law reform bill.[11]

Corporations bolster their images on Capitol Hill by providing constituents legislative information. For example, Penney's and Sears Roebuck asked their store managers to write letters to their representatives about a bill that would increase the ability of individuals to initiate class-action suits. They argued that if such suits were allowed, the courts would be jammed with irresponsible litigation benefitting gun-slinging lawyers seeking riches through the naïveté of legitimate businesses. The provision was defeated.[12]

Other Answers

Corporate PACs and lobbying efforts are the two major means business uses to safeguard its public image. Other creative channels are also being employed.

One means is continued communication between the corporation and its employees. Many corporations run educational seminars for managers to inform them about political issues and instruct them on ways to run and influence political campaigns. Government representatives are brought into the company to teach seminars and to communicate with managers about relevant issues.

Another means for safeguarding the public image is issues management analysis. The function of this activity is to produce position papers, or white papers, on issues affecting the corporation. These papers are written by government issues departments within companies. ARCO maintains a governmental issues section which helps company representatives sort through legislation and speak with one voice. Its staff studies and tracks legislation in issue clusters and lends support in developing company positions on pertinent topics, such as public lands policy, national health care, and hazardous and toxic substances.

In addition, companies with similar interests are forming coalitions to support mutual concerns. The coalition may be built around a specific piece of legislation, and unions and other outside interest groups may join the coalition. The ultimate objective is to mobilize allies with the capability of tapping into resources and support on issues.

IMPROVING PUBLIC PERCEPTION ABOUT GOVERNMENT/BUSINESS RELATIONS

If business and government have traditionally been at odds with one another, it is perhaps ironic that while attempting to improve that relationship business has suffered a loss of image. *PACs* and *lobbyists* are two words which generate public distaste. Perhaps it is natural that the public views business/government interaction with skepticism. Yet the need for interaction between government and business is increasing. As consumers insist on protection from products which harm health, the government must become involved. And as employees insist on fair labor laws and safe work conditions, the government must become involved in the business of businesses. The obvious thing lacking, then, is to make the public understand that government/business interaction is not only necessary but beneficial to employees, consumers, investors, and the public as a whole. Perhaps more than any other area in forming positive corporate images, business has been particularly amiss in addressing public misconceptions about government/business relations. As corporate executives come to realize the need for educating the public about government/business interaction, the misconception will be corrected.

NOTES

1. William R. Doerner, "Of PACs and Campaign Pledges," *Time* (May 7, 1984): 24.

2. *Public Relations Journal* (August 1983).

3. Ibid.

4. Craig E. Aranoff and Otis W. Baskin, *Public Relations: The Profession and the Practice* (St. Paul, Minn.: West Publishing Co., 1983), p. 338.

5. Ibid., p. 339.

6. From a telephone interview with Raymond Hoewing, vice president, Public Affairs Council, May 1984. Subsequent references to Hoewing's statements are taken from this interview.

7. Ibid.

8. Aranoff and Baskin, p. 351.

9. Ibid., p. 345.

10. From a telephone interview with Irene M. Brandt, government relations representative, Eli Lilly & Co., June 1984.

11. Aranoff and Baskin, p. 346.

12. Ibid., p. 247.

PART III

Measuring Impact

12

Thoughts About Corporate Image: A Corporate Image Survey

After reading this book, you should now be ready to put together an image of your corporation. Your thoughts are stimulated about your standing with the various publics your company does business with and the way these publics perceive your company.

The purposes of this final chapter are twofold. The first section provides a thought-provoking list of questions to help you form a nonscientific corporate image profile. The second section provides a capsule summary of publics and possible corporate objectives to be gained with each public. Media methods and the resulting effects tie together the image-enhancement effort.

Guidelines to form your own corporate image profile are saved for this last chapter. Profiling your corporation's image is a continuous process. It has no beginning nor end, but demands constant thought and evaluation. Like individual personalities, there are as many images as there are companies, and any influence acting upon them affects the picture.

The guidelines presented here pull together information provided in the preceding chapters to form your own corporate image profile. These hints serve to provoke continued thinking about your company image and offer considerations for amending that image.

The guidelines presented in this summary chapter are intended to be more thought-provoking than scientific. A number of companies offer scientific image surveys. Opinion Research Corporation, Roper Public Opinion Research Center, Inc., Louis Harris and Associates, Yankelovich, Skelly and White are among many which offer such services. Their advice may well be worth the investment. Seeking the advice of an image consultant is another alternative.

SELF-HELP SURVEY

Answer the following questions with a *yes* or *no* response.

Your Corporate Image

1. Overall, are you dissatisfied with your present corporate image?
2. Do you employ a firm to:
   a. design logos?
   b. promote your image?
   c. run a public relations campaign?
   d. develop promotional literature?
3. Have you established clear objectives about what you want your image to convey?
4. Have you set reasonable budget limitations to promote your image?
5. Will your public relations firm work with you to analyze the marketplace and promote your organization aggressively?
6. Does everyone in your organization approve of, understand, and support your present image?
7. Does your corporation set specific social goals in addition to corporate goals?
8. Have you determined who your important publics are?
9. Have you surveyed various publics about your corporate image?
10. Are you comfortable about the public view of your corporate image?
11. Does your organization reevaluate its image periodically to make sure it is still on track?

Your Corporate Name

1. Does your corporate name reflect your organization's products or services?
2. Is the name easy to pronounce and easily understood on the telephone?
3. Is the name easy to spell?
4. Does the name look good on stationery, signs, and other appropriate symbols?
5. Does the name look good with its logo?
6. Does the name reflect the geographic areas where your corporation operates?
7. Is the name free of racial, ethnic, or sexual bias?
8. Is the name free of confusion with other corporate names?
9. Does the name convey success?
10. Does the name have distinction?
11. Is the name short and simple enough to be easily understood?
12. Has the name been registered?

Your Corporate Logo

1. Does your logo look:
   a. upbeat?
   b. contemporary?
   c. flexible?
   d. dynamic?

2. Does the logo reflect the product and service you sell?
3. Does it show imagination?
4. Does the logo show the geographic scope of your business?
5. Is it easy to remember?
6. Is it appealing?
7. Does it give rise to positive emotions?
8. Does your logo show up well:
   a. in black-and-white newsprint?
   b. in full color?
   c. on signs?
   d. in promotional literature?

Your Corporate Management

1. Does management promote your corporate image?
2. Does management send clear signals about economic and social corporate goals to:
   a. employees?
   b. the community?
   c. consumers?
3. Are managers professional in dealing with:
   a. employees?
   b. the community?
   c. consumers?
4. Do managers know about and fully use media sources to promote corporate image?
5. Are your corporate leaders and managers active in:
   a. professional associations?
   b. community social and civic groups?
   c. political and governmental affairs?
   d. other organizations which help promote image?
6. Does management attempt to help employees understand their jobs as part of the total corporate mission?
7. Does your company finance outside training and education?
8. Does your company bring experts, consultants, trainers, and speakers in-house to address or work with employees?
9. Are yardsticks in place to select corporate spokespersons?
10. Does management support quality in product and service offerings?

Your Corporate Communications Office

1. Does your organization maintain a central communications or media office?
2. Is the office well staffed with a manager, government relations officer, writers, spokespersons, and sufficient clerical support?
3. Does it handle media such as:
   a. press releases?
   b. news conferences?
   c. promotional literature?
   d. approving interviews to the press?

4. Is newsworthy information fed into this office through an established network?
5. Are lines of communication open between this office and:
   a. state and local corporate officers?
   b. community organizations?
6. Is this media office prepared or can it respond quickly to crisis situations?
7. Does the media office handle the press openly, honestly, and consistently?
8. Can your media office personnel handle live television conferences, briefings, or interviews?
9. Do stories or information clear the media office so that a single and consistent viewpoint is relayed to the media?
10. Does your media office maintain up-to-date information?
11. Does your communications office actively seek contact with the local media?
12. Does your communications office keep local media informed?
13. Does your communications office maintain a conference room or area for media events, especially press conferences?
14. Is the news conference room well equipped with sufficient lighting, outlets, a platform, chairs, microphones, etc.?
15. Do your communications office personnel provide reporters with sample products, blueprints showing expansion, black-and-white glossies, or other supplementary materials?
16. Are your spokespersons well prepared to appear on televison?
17. Have they received media training such as a television preparation seminar?
18. Are corporate spokespersons guided to present a single stance when appearing on television or when heard in radio interview broadcasts?
19. Do corporate spokespersons consistently relay a basic message which appears single-purposed and to the point?

Corporate Employees

1. Do your corporate objectives encourage interaction between management and employees?
2. Does your organization promote communications through media such as employee newsletters?
3. Does your organization insist that management maintain an open-door policy and remain accessible to employees?
4. Does your organization keep employees informed about objectives, plans, policies, and procedures?
5. Does your organization encourage employee feedback and suggestions?
6. Does your organization respond quickly and decisively to safety and health hazards?
7. Is your organization honest and open with employees about sensitive and controversial issues?
8. Does your organization communicate important events and decisions to employees?
9. Does your organization urge innovation and creativity among employees?
10. Would you describe overall labor/management relations in your organization as healthy?

11. Does your organization provide or sponsor training programs for employees?
12. Does your organization reward employees for meritorious service related either to work or community activities?
13. Does your organization maintain a new-employee orientation program?
14. Does your organization communicate its fair labor practices to employees and the community?
15. Does your organization offer stock options, profit sharing, or other benefits to employees?
16. Does your organization offer competitive salaries and benefits?

Community Relations

1. Is your organization involved in conservation of community natural resources?
2. Overall, do your organization's policies and practices promote sound community relations?
3. Is your organization sensitive to community concerns such as waste disposal; area unemployment; needs of minority groups; adequate housing, parks, schools, and colleges; noise and traffic problems; and natural resources limitations?
4. Has your organization established sound relations with local and state government leaders?
5. Does your organization maintain channels of communication with the community?
6. Does your organization hold annual open houses to encourage community members to become acquainted with your facilities, products, and services?
7. Does your organization patronize local merchants?
8. Does your organization sponsor, contribute to, or donate expertise, funds, products, services, or time to charitable, civic, educational, or political groups?
9. Are your corporate leaders involved in local, civic, and social organizations?
10. Does your organization encourage employees and corporate leaders to participate in local community volunteer programs?

Consumer Trust

1. Does your company have a customer relations department?
2. Does your company have in place a program that spells out how to handle customer complaints?
3. Does your company keep a customer complaint log?
4. Does your company analyze the complaint log for recurring complaints and developing patterns?
5. Does your company respond immediately, courteously, and decisively to customer complaints?
6. Does your company monitor personnel who respond to customers?
7. Does your company train employees in how to handle customers?
8. Has your organization developed a slogan or theme to convey your goals to customers?

Government Relations

1. Does someone in your organization deal with government issues?
2. Do members of your organization meet with government officials on issues relevant to the company?
3. Do members of your organization maintain contact with government officials in Washington, D.C.?
4. Do you encourage corporate or employee membership in PACs?
5. Is your organization represented by lobbyists in state and federal governments?

Keeping Score

After answering the survey, review your tallied responses by sections. Record them on the score card below:

12.1
Score Card

	No. of Yes Responses	No. of No Responses	Total Responses
Overall Corporate Image			14
Corporate Name			12
Corporate Logo			14
Corporate Management			17
Corporate Communications Office			23
Corporate Employees			16
Community Relations			10
Consumer Trust			8
Government Relations			5

Now that you have completed the survey with a *yes* or a *no* response, tally the total number of positives and negatives. The questions are structured so that a *yes* response means you are taking positive actions to promote a favorable corporate image. Negative responses mean you have room for improvement.

Figure the percentage of *yes* and *no* responses for each topic area. If you responded negatively to a majority of questions under a particular heading, this may be an indication that your corporate image is weak in that area. For example, if the *yes* responses were high in consumer relations but low in employee relations, you will want to review your employee program to bolster your image efforts.

To begin, go back to the particular section (e.g., employee relations) and write out answers to the questions posed. Your written answer lends further definition to pinpoint specific weaknesses.

Reread the chapter that corresponds to the problem area. If you feel the problem warrants, you may want to seek the advice of a consultant.

THE POWER OF PUBLICS

The various publics you must address in establishing a corporate image wield great power. To underestimate their powers can be an error as grave as ignoring smoke before a fire. Danger still exists even though the smoke doesn't burn you. The various publics a corporation must contend with are, first and foremost, the corporate family—its employees; its immediate environment—the community; the people it serves—its customers; and the various governments within which it operates.

Corporate leaders are coming to realize that each of these publics must be dealt with in different ways. Each public has its own interests and its own needs. And the lines of communication from the corporation to the various publics differ. Each is important in its own way, so that priorities cannot be set by allowing one public to take precedence over another. Above all, corporate leaders are realizing that they must give each of these publics individual consideration and attention.

Corporations can no longer ignore social responsibility. They can no longer afford to target profit motive as their only objective. And they can no longer tolerate negative public views which drive wedges between what the company is and what the public *thinks* it is. It is no accident that we see many commercials on television and in magazines which in no way attempt to offer a product. Instead, many commercials are simply selling the image of the entire organization. Audiences are not asked, for instance, to buy an IBM computer. They are asked to like IBM.

IMAGE AS A MANAGEMENT PRIORITY

In my previous book, *The Winning Image*, I devoted a section to "refocusing" the personal image. As the adage goes, the only certainty in life is change. However, most business environments are conservative and many businessmen distrust sudden, drastic change. They prefer gradual changes put to the test of time. Gradual changes allow room for the adjustments, and adjustment is easier.

Ralph Waldo Emerson, writing in *Self-Reliance*, advises us to "avoid appearances." In *The Winning Image*, I advised avoiding a cosmetic appearance change. There must be substance to reinforce the outward appearance of corporate image. Similarly, when a change of corporate image is involved, the appearance of logos, stationery, and signs will mean little if underlying forces at work with the media and other publics are not readily apparent.

Public relations professionals are familiar with the four-step process that makes up an award-winning campaign: research, planning, communicating, and evaluation. *The Corporate Image* deals primarily with the third of these, communicating the corporate image. But some attention must be given to steps one and two before communication can be implemented.

Your organization may go so far as to hire professional pollsters or consultants to complete the research step for you. Often this alliance produces a more objective viewpoint than that of managers and executives from within the organization. Managers tend to express themselves more openly with outsiders also. Self-examination, be it personal or corporate, is often eye-opening. The key is critical self-examination and constructive criticism.

The first questions asked in changing a personal image concern evaluating the present image. What are its weaknesses and its strengths? Central to that answer is perception versus reality. The change demands examination both internally and externally.

Benefits from Improved Image

Just as examination must include external and internal review, an improved image offers external and internal benefits. Internal benefits include management's clear perception of company goals, high employee morale, the attraction of quality personnel, increased focus for communications, provision of quality products and services, and greater efficiency.

External benefits include a coordinated media picture, consumer awareness of product quality and strengths in management, competitive products and services, financial and investment opportunities, well-defined business objectives, community and government support, and most of all a corporate image which the public perceives as responsible, dependable, and trustworthy.

Table 12-2 summarizes these benefits and shows how best to achieve them. Many strategies exist which promote a corporate identity. A well-organized program penetrates an entire organization from employees through investors. The net result from such a program will be improved standing in the local community, in the business world, and in the world of public scrutiny as a whole. All this translates into profitability, growth, prosperity, and a corporation which has the respect of the many publics it encounters.

12.2
Effects Achieved with Comprehensive Image-Building Program

Publics	Corporate Objectives	Media Methods	Effects
Internal			
Employees	Maintain management/employee communications	Hold employee meetings	Improve employee morale
	Maintain skilled labor	Hold employee/supervisor conferences	Improve customer and community relations due to high morale
	Produce quality products and services	Notify employees of policy changes	Improve corporate image among employees
	Ensure employee health and safety	Publish newsletter and other employee communications	Attract and keep quality people
		Promote skills training among employees	Increase profits
		Provide competitive salaries, benefits, bonuses, and other rewards	Provide quality products and services
		Provide encouragement through verbal praise and commendation	Increase productivity
		Train employees in health and safety	Maintain good workers' safety record
External			
Community	Gain community support	Promote news features and advertise in local newspapers	Gain community support of company objectives
		Patronize community businesses	Improve community housing, schools, and resources
		Establish rapport with community media	Improve corporate image in community

12.2
Effects Achieved with Comprehensive Image-Building Program (continued)

Publics	Corporate Objectives	Media Methods	Effects
External			
		Join community organizations	Increase knowledge in the community as to how the company fits in and supports the community
		Hold open houses	
		Donate to community charities and schools	
		Take active role in developing community resources	
		Get corporate leaders involved in community social and civic groups	
		Involve corporate leaders in local and state government	
Consumers	Ensure profit	Provide quality products and services	Gain public confidence in products and services
	Minimize consumer complaints	Gain reputation for reliability	Gain profitability, growth
		Ensure honest labeling and advertising claims	Avoid damage to corporate image during crises
		Remain aware of consumer needs	Improve corporate image among consumers
		Ensure consumer health and safety	
		Handle consumer complaints promptly, courteously, and efficiently	
		Promote name, logo, and slogan	

Publics	Corporate Objectives	Media Methods	Effects
External			
Government	Maintain healthy government relations	Comply with government regulations	Stay abreast of government regulations
		Establish PACs	Improve corporate/ government relations
		Establish lobbyist groups	
		Establish rapport with local, state, and federal governments	

Index

About the Author

James Gray, Jr., Media Impact owner and principal consultant, is a founding leader in the media and image consulting field. In business for over a decade, his career spans training, college teaching, and writing.

Gray designs and conducts seminars for business, government, and education. Among his client roster are senators, Congresspeople, political office seekers, and executives from Xerox, Boeing, NBC, AT&T, and the Pentagon.

Gray is the author of *The Winning Image*, a contributing author to *Image Impact for Men*, and his magazine and newspaper features include *Time, The Washington Post, The Journal of Campaigns and Elections, United Airlines,* and *Richmond News Leader*. A well-known media personality, Gray is a frequent television and radio talk show guest.

A former faculty member of The School of Communication, The American University, Washington, D.C., Gray conducts professional development seminars for its Office of Continuing Education. Nominated to *Who's Who in the East,* Gray also belongs to The American Society for Training and Development.